Sean McD

Think
Biblically

Addressing Cultural Issues
with **Clarity** and **Boldness**

Editorial Team

Timothy Fox
Writer

Kyle Wiltshire
Content Editor

Jennifer Siao
Production Editor

Shiloh Stufflebeam
Graphic Designer

Karen Daniel
Editorial Team Leader

John Paul Basham
Manager, Student Ministry Publishing

Ben Trueblood
Director, Student Ministry

Published by Lifeway Press® • © Sean McDowell 2022

ISBN: 978-1-0877-5248-8

Item: 005834430

Dewey Decimal Classification Number: 248.83

Subject Heading: CHRISTIANITY/CHRISTIAN ETHICS (MORAL THEOLOGY)/SPECIFIC MORAL ISSUES

Printed in the United States of America.

Student Ministry Publishing
Lifeway Resources
200 Powell Place, Suite 100
Brentwood, TN 37027

Contents

About the Author — 04

Guide — 06

A Note From the Author — 07

Session 1: How to Take a Stand — 08

Session 2: Relationships — 22

Session 3: Sex — 36

Session 4: Care — 50

Session 5: Culture — 64

Session 6: How to Love Your Neighbor — 78

Tips for Leading a Group — 93

Leader Guide — 94

About the Author

DR. SEAN MCDOWELL is a gifted communicator with a passion for equipping the church, and in particular young people, to make the case for the Christian faith. He connects with audiences in a tangible way through humor and stories while imparting hard evidence and logical support for viewing all areas of life through a Biblical worldview. Sean is an Associate Professor in the Christian Apologetics program at Talbot School of Theology, Biola University.

Sean also teaches a high school Bible class, which helps give him exceptional insight into the prevailing culture so he can impart his observations poignantly to fellow educators, pastors, and parents alike. In 2008 he received the Educator of the Year award for San Juan Capistrano, California. The Association of Christian Schools International awarded Exemplary Status to his apologetics training. Sean is listed among the top 100 apologists. He graduated summa cum laude from Talbot Theological Seminary with a double master's degree in Theology and Philosophy. He earned a Ph.D. in Apologetics and Worldview Studies from Southern Baptist Theological Seminary in 2014.

Traveling throughout the United States and abroad, Sean speaks at camps, churches, schools, universities, and conferences. He has spoken for organizations including Focus on the Family, the Chuck Colson Center for Christian Worldview, Cru, Youth Specialties, Hume Lake Christian Camps, Fellowship of Christian Athletes and the Association of Christian Schools International. Sean is the co-host for the Think Biblically podcast, which is one of the most popular podcasts on faith and cultural engagement. Sean's YouTube channel (Dr. Sean McDowell) is one of the top apologetics channels.

Sean is the author, co-author, or editor of over twenty books including *Chasing Love, The Fate of the Apostles, So The Next Generation Will Know* (with J. Warner Wallace), *Evidence that Demands a Verdict* (with Josh McDowell), *Same-Sex Marriage: A Thoughtful Approach to God's Design for Marriage* (with John Stonestreet), *Is God Just a Human Invention?* (with Jonathan Morrow) and *Understanding Intelligent Design* (with William A. Dembski). Sean is the General Editor for A New Kind of Apologist, Apologetics for a New Generation, Sharing the Good News with Mormons, and The Apologetics Study Bible for Students. Sean has one of the leading apologetics blogs, which can be read at seanmcdowell.org.

In April 2000, Sean married his high school sweetheart, Stephanie. They have three children and live in San Juan Capistrano, California. Sean played college basketball at Biola University and was the captain his senior year on a team that went 30-7.

This Bible study book includes six weeks of content. Each week has video teaching, followed by content designed for groups and individuals.

GROUP DISCUSSION

Begin each week with the group discussion. This section uses the following format to facilitate simple yet meaningful interaction among group members, with God's Word and with the video teaching.

WATCH

Video content can be found at lifeway.com/thinkbiblically. Each video is 6-8 minutes long and designed to help students think about the topics for the week and engage in discussion. There is a guide that includes key points from the video teaching with blanks for students to fill in as they watch the video.

DISCUSS

These pages include questions and statements that guide students to respond to the video teaching and to relevant Bible passages. Since this study covers difficult topics, it's important to consider the age, maturity level, and needs of your group. Consult with church leadership and parents about any controversial questions that may be covered during group time.

PERSONAL STUDY

Four days of personal study are provided each week to take students deeper into Scripture and to supplement the biblical truths introduced in the group discussion and teaching time. These pages challenge students to grow in their understanding of God's Word and to make practical applications to their lives.

LEADER GUIDE

At the back of the book is a leader guide to help you walk students through these challenging topics. There you will find an icebreaker, discussion tips, and prayer prompts to go along with the discussion guide found in each session.

A Note From the Author

We live in one of the most divided times in American history. How can Christians stand up for truth and justice, and yet do it in a loving, God-honoring way? This is exactly the question we are going to explore in this study.

Despite what many people think, there is a way to have civil, meaningful conversations with people about issues that matter. The key is being thoughtful about our own beliefs and learning some tools for engaging others. This study will help you do both.

This study will also help you explore biblical principles for how to think about some of the most controversial issues of our day. Obviously, what you'll find here is not exhaustive, but it will give you a great place to begin to think biblically about these important topics. You will also be equipped with some ideas for how to put the knowledge you gain into action, so you can have a positive influence on others for the sake of the kingdom of God.

Let's go!

Session 1

How To Take a Stand

WATCH

Use the fill-in-the-blanks and note-taking space as you watch the Session 1 teaching video together as a group.

Sean says he wants to motivate you to be like this through this study:

Someone with _____ , willing to do the right thing, ___ _____

_____ ____ _____ may be.

> **Read Daniel 1:8a (CSB).**

"Daniel determined that he would not defile himself with the king's food ..."

A reason you might get defensive:

Maybe you _____ _____what you believe and why you believe it.

Response to Sean from atheist:

"I'm _____ they'll treat me like they just treated you."

The two goals of this study are:

Goal 1: Think biblically about _____.

Goal 2: Be motivated by _____.

> **Read John 13:35 (CSB).**

"By this everyone will know that you are my disciples, if you love one another."

Teaching videos are available at lifeway.com/thinkbiblically

Jessica never imagined she would be facing the decision that was before her today. Growing up in church, she had learned much about making right choices in the areas of sex, love, and relationships, but this was beyond anything she had been tested with before. "How can I possibly do the right thing," she wondered, "when my college psychology professor has assigned me to review a porn film as part of my grade?" Without this assignment Jessica's grade would suffer greatly, but she also knew that God wanted her to be sexually pure.

What could she do in this situation?

What would you do?

Jaelene faced one of the toughest decisions of her life. Would she wear a U.S. national soccer team jersey sporting rainbow numbers to celebrate gay pride? Or should she decline, and jeopardize her position on the team? You might not think this is such a big deal. After all, it's just a jersey, right? Because of her Christian faith, and her convictions about God's design for sex and marriage, it was a big deal for Jaelene. Choosing not to wear the jersey might cost her a spot on the team?

What should she do?

What would you do?

These are both true stories and scenarios young people who are followers of Jesus, like yourself, have faced. They are not easy situations to be in. Can you imagine the pressure they'd feel to compromise their Christian convictions? After all, both worked hard for their success. Jessica and Jaelene want to excel in life and they also want to honor the Lord. Is there a way to do both? Should they really be expected to suffer for doing the right thing? Doesn't God want them to be happy?

Every day you face moral choices: Will I respect my parents? Should I post that on social media? How far should I go with my boyfriend or girlfriend? Will I use the preferred gender pronoun for a classmate? Should I join a protest for climate change, racial reconciliation, immigration, or some other pressing issue?

What are the issues that concern you the most, and why?

The question is not if you will face challenging situations like Jessica or Jaelene, but when will you face them. How you respond to moral dilemmas reflects who you are right now and, in turn, shapes who you become. This is all the more important for those who want to follow Jesus. Since He calls His people to live in a different way than the world around us, that means a lot of the thinking and acting the world calls moral is not only unhelpful, but often harmful. The purpose of this study is to equip you to think through some of today's most pressing ethical issues so you can be a faithful follower of Jesus.

Even though you are a young Christian, I believe God can use you right now to make a difference.

Do you really believe this? Why or why not?

You may feel so overwhelmed with your responsibilities and the number of moral issues you are expected to have an opinion about, that you feel like you hardly have time to slow down and grow up. Bombarded by endless worldly messages of compromise, who can honestly expect you to make right choices today?

The answer to that question is simple: God does. God expects you to make right choices. God's standards never change–even if ours do. God not only expects you to stand up for what is right, He will empower you with the strength to do so. How can you possibly do that today? Let's start by looking back at the story of Daniel, a young man who stood boldly for what was right in his day.

Give students a few minutes to read Daniel 1.

Daniel was an exile from Jerusalem, forced to live in Babylon, after his people were conquered. He could interpret dreams, he survived a night in a lion's den, and he faced many tough decisions.

In Daniel 1:3-4, King Nebuchadnezzar assigned Ashpenaz, his chief eunuch, to select smart, handsome, and noble young men from among the exiles. They were to learn the language, literature, and traditions of the Babylonians for three years so they could serve in the king's palace. There was one big problem for Daniel and his friends: In order to fulfill these duties, they had to accept the royal food and drink, which violated the law God had prescribed for His people to follow. Daniel and his friends had a tough decision: Would they seek to please the king or honor God? Daniel came up with a creative solution, which ended up honoring God and the king.

> **Read Daniel 1:8.**

But Daniel resolved that he would not defile himself with the king's food, or with the wine that he drank.

What is significant about Daniel's attitude?

The word "resolved" is past tense. In other words, even before Daniel knew the outcome, he determined he was going to honor God. He refused to defile his body even before he knew what the outcome would be. Now that's conviction.

Do you have a "Daniel dilemma" in your life, in which you feel caught in a tug-of-war between God and your friends, family, or school? If so, would you mind sharing it with the group?

Determining that you want to honor the Lord before moral challenges come is important for standing strong today. It is often too late—although not impossible—to do the right thing without developing convictions beforehand. Have you done that? Have you resolved, like Daniel, to honor God regardless of the cost?

I can't make this decision for you and neither can your parents. Only you can make it. If you do, I can't promise that your life will be easier. The apostle Peter indicated that it may be God's will for believers to suffer (1 Pet. 3:17). In the case of Jessica, things did work out well. After prayer and counsel, she proposed to her teacher that he allow her to write a persuasive paper on why she should be excused from the assignment. He reluctantly agreed.

She wrote a four-page paper on why, as a Christian, she should not watch pornography. Can you guess what happened? Not only did he accept the paper, but he also had her present it to the entire class and allowed other students to opt out of the assignment as well. Nearly half the class followed her lead. One person can make a difference.

Jaelene was not so fortunate. After three days of prayer and reflection, she chose to withdraw from the women's national team rather than wear the jersey supporting gay pride. "If I never get another national team call-up again then that's just a part of His plan, and that's okay," she said. "Maybe this is why I was meant to play soccer, to show other believers to be obedient."[1]

She was arguably the best fullback in the game at the time of the U.S. Women's World Cup tryout, and yet because of her convictions, she wasn't given a slot on the roster. She regularly receives jeers and boos when she plays in the National Women's Soccer League. For Jaelene, doing the right thing cost her dearly.

What do the different outcomes of each situation teach you about the moral decisions you will make in life?

Although different outcomes, both Jessica and Jaelene chose wisely. They both honored the Lord, like Daniel, regardless of the consequences.

Will you?

Day 1:
WHO ARE YOU TO JUDGE?

Not long ago, while speaking on moral issues with a youth group, a teen girl stood up and asked: "Who are you to judge?" She clearly thought I was being hateful for claiming certain behaviors as wrong.

How would you respond to her if she asked you the same question about a pressing moral issue?

As best as I can remember, I simply said, "I have thought about this for a long time, weighed all sides of the issue, and think my position is the most moral, although I am open to correction if you could show where I am wrong." She wasn't quite sure how to respond.

My goal wasn't to embarrass her, but to point out that as human beings and followers of Jesus, we are supposed to make informed moral judgments. We do it all the time. In fact, ironically, she was morally judging me! By asking what right I had to make a moral judgment, she was implying that I should not make such a judgment. But isn't that a judgment? Of course!

Without realizing it, people regularly say contradictory things like this. Try to see what is wrong with the following statements:

"You should be tolerant of views different than your own."

"You should not force your morals on others."

"It is arrogant to think you are right."

Each one of these examples make a claim that contradicts itself. Many times when someone says, "You should be tolerant of other views" what they mean is, "You should be tolerant of my views, but I don't have to be tolerant of your views."

Though many people may say moral claims are not grounded in absolute truth and are simply personal preference, that thought is a claim for absolute truth. Whether people acknowledge it or not, truth is hardwired into our hearts.

Consider Romans 2:14: "For when Gentiles, who do not have the law, by nature do what the law requires, they are a law to themselves."

When have you seen an example of people who do not believe in God following His law?

According to Paul, God has made all human beings with a moral conscience to recognize right and wrong. Thus, even people who do not even believe in God are still made in His image and recognize right and wrong. Even atheists can be moral because God's law is written on their hearts.

Let's go back to the idea of judgment. You might ask, "Didn't Jesus tell us not to judge?" In Matthew 7:1 (NIV), Jesus said, "Do not judge, or you too will be judged." That's true, but look at the fuller context of His teaching. In verse 5, He said, "first take the plank out of your own eye, and then you will see clearly to remove the speck from your brother's eye."

What is the real problem Jesus was addressing?

Jesus wasn't saying never to make moral judgments. What He was teaching against was hypocritical judgment, where we judge others with a standard we do not apply to ourselves. Before we can criticize someone else's faults, we need to examine our own first. When we've examined our own heart in view of God's Word, then we can help others come to an understanding of His truth.

Day 2:
HOW DO I BECOME A GOOD PERSON?

Why do people have opinions on issues?

What factors cause someone to adopt an opinion as their own?

People claim an opinion on something because they believe it is right. Most people take a side because they believe it is good and decent. Today more than ever, people want to be on the "right side of history." But how do you know what is good and right and become a good person?

The choices we make are an extension of who we are. We don't make moral choices in isolation from our character, and we don't make good choices by accident. If we want to make right choices, we have to develop certain virtues into our lives.

How do we do this?

1. **Repent of your sins and believe in Jesus. Becoming the kind of person God wants us to be begins by recognizing our own failed attempts at being good, so that we will repent of our sins and trust Jesus to transform us through His grace.**

   How have you seen Jesus transform you through His grace?

2. Saturate yourself in Scripture. Paul said to not "be conformed to this world, but be transformed by the renewal of your mind" (Rom. 12:2a). One of the most important ways to avoid conforming to this world, and to experience transformation, is to study God's Word.

    How has God's Word helped you transform into the person God wants you to be?

3. Be a person of prayer.

    Why is prayer so important?

Prayer is not primarily about getting things from God. It is about conforming our will to His. We pray for our enemies so we can better love them. We pray for those who persecute us so that God will change our hearts. Prayer is essential for becoming a person who is truly capable of loving his or her neighbor.

4. Choose friends wisely.

    How do you choose your friends?

    How much do your friends influence you?

There are few people in life who will have a bigger impact on you than your friends. Good friends not only keep us from trouble, they help us live wise and courageous lives. This is why it's so important to be a member of a local church. God has designed the church as a means through which believers are discipled, counseled, supported, and encouraged. Join a good church and get involved!

Day 3:
HOW DO I LOVE MY NEIGHBOR?

At churches, conferences, and schools, I often role-play an atheist to motivate Christians to see how prepared (or unprepared) they are to engage someone who doesn't believe the same way we do. While audiences know I am really a Christian, I put on glasses to "become" an atheist character, take live questions from the audience, and then offer my best atheist responses.

After I have offered some thoughtful atheist responses, groups often get defensive. I have had people storm out of the session, yell answers across the room, and personally insult me. And they know I'm role-playing!

Why do you think some Christians respond this way?

I am convinced there are two big reasons.

1. **Many Christians don't know what they believe and why. If we don't have solid reasons for our beliefs, it is difficult to respond graciously when people challenge us.**

    How do you respond when someone challenges what you believe?

2. **We forget how gracious God has been toward us. When someone is transformed by God's mercy, they will extend mercy to others. Therefore, a failure to grant mercy to others reveals we don't truly grasp the depth of God's mercy to us.**

How do you know you have experienced God's grace personally?

One reason it is so challenging to love our neighbors today is that our culture operates under a different definition of love than what Jesus teaches.

How does our culture define love?

Today, love means affirming someone's behavior and beliefs. It means accepting someone for who they believe themselves to be. And it means agreeing with however someone feels about themselves. If not, you're considered to be hateful.

How does Jesus define love?

Love involves a willingness to sacrifice for the good of another. It is a commitment to the well-being of another person, even if he or she does not recognize or accept the reality of the good. Biblically, love involves being committed to what God says is good for someone, regardless of how they feel.

With this in mind, how can you better love your neighbor today?

It is not easy to love your neighbor today. In reality, it never has been easy to follow in the steps of Jesus. But God has called you to this task. Are you up for the challenge?

Day 4:
WHAT IS MY WORLDVIEW?

One of the most significant lessons my dad has taught me is about the power of assumptions. As a high school student, I remember him saying, "When you read an article or book, always discern the assumptions of the person who wrote it. Their assumptions will shape everything they write." Although it took me some time to really grasp its significance, now I see how powerful this insight is.

Essentially, my dad was teaching me to understand the power of worldview. Simply put, a worldview is the way we see the world. It is how we perceive reality and the filter through which we see the world.

What are three elements that shape your worldview?

Worldviews answer big questions like: Is there a God? Does life continue after death? What is a human being? What brings true happiness? Is there a moral law?

Take some time to think about these questions. How does the Bible answer them? Write down your answers below and include a verse or two as evidence.

Is there a God?

Does life continue after death?

What is a human being?

Is there a moral law?

Everyone has a worldview. They may not know what it's called, but ideas shape what people think and believe.

HERE ARE A FEW PROMINENT WORLDVIEWS AND BRIEF EXPLANATIONS OF THEM:

- **Naturalism is the idea that God does not exist and that everything can be explained by natural forces.**

- **Secular humanism is a naturalist worldview that states truth and goodness can be discovered apart from religion or God.**

- **Existentialism is a naturalist worldview based on the idea that humans define our own existence.**

- **Consumerism says you are what you own and promises happiness to those who have things.**

- **Hedonism considers the pursuit of pleasure the highest good.**

- **Individualism places the individual at the center of moral authority.**

Not only are each of these worldviews in conflict with the teachings of Jesus, they also profoundly shape the life choices of those who hold them.

How do you recognize worldviews? Here are a few pointers:

- **When reading a book, article, or social media post, consider a few questions: Who is the author? What is his or her expertise? Who is he or she writing to and why? What is his or her belief system? Consider the same kinds of questions when watching television or videos on social media platforms.**

- **When having a conversation, ask probing questions and be a good listener. Try to discern the underlying assumptions driving the person's moral beliefs or behavior.**

Learning to recognize underlying worldviews is an important skill for Christians who want to be able to engage people around them in meaningful conversations. Understanding our own worldview helps us think biblically.

Session 2

Relationships

WATCH

Use the fill-in-the-blanks and note-taking space as you watch the Session 2 teaching video together as a group.

As we begin to discuss the topic of race, let's consider these things:

Biblically we're called to begin with _____ and _____.

The Bible values _____.

God values race in the past.

God values race in the present.

There is no movement or organization in the world with more _____

_____ than the _____.

God values race in the future (Rev. 7:9-10).

How do we move forward to best love our neighbors:

> **Read James 1:19b (NIV).**

"...Everyone should be quick to listen, slow to speak..."

Just _____.

Teaching videos are available at lifeway.com/thinkbiblically

Your parents and grandparents will remember the tragic events of 9/11 well. As we look back on that tragic day, something interesting stands out: No one grieves for the buildings. Regardless of how majestic and expensive they were, people do not mourn the loss of the buildings. From the moment of the attack, we mourned the thousands of lives lost. We mourn the deaths of fathers, mothers, friends, firemen, children, and others who died on that terrible day. Why? Because it is people who matter most.

Have you ever suffered great tragedy in life? If so, what is the first thing you did and why?

Tragedy does not cause us to value people more; it reveals what we already value. We value people and we desire to be in healthy, meaningful relationships with others. We desire to love and be loved. It isn't that school, activities, or personal belongings do not matter at all, but that people matter more.

Why do we value people so much?

According to the worldview of naturalism—the belief that the natural world is all that exists—humans are just a cosmic accident; the product of a purposeless process. We hold no special value but are just tiny specks living on a small blue dot somewhere within a vast universe. And the universe certainly does not know or care that we exist. This is a very atheistic perspective. Now, this is not to say that atheists do not or cannot value humans. Most do! But according to the worldview of naturalism, humans are not special.

Even though humans hold no special value according to naturalistic atheism, why do atheists know deep down that people are valuable?

Why are humans valuable according to Christianity?

Let's contrast naturalism with Christianity. The Bible teaches that humans have immense value, having been created in the image of God (Gen. 1:27). God loved us so much that even when we were still sinners, He sent His Son to die for us (Rom. 5:8). We're valuable because God made us as the pinnacle of creation. The beauty of grounding our value in being created in God's image is that we can't do anything to lose it. Nor can we do anything to gain it.

How does it make you feel to know that nothing we do can ever add to or decrease from our value?

When we form our identity through other, lesser things such as our appearance, accomplishments, grades, or the number of followers we have on social media, we get into trouble. These things are all counterfeits that won't ultimately fill our hearts with meaning. Over time, pursuing such things only makes us feel less attractive or less valuable. The Bible teaches that we are to love God first and others second. Trying to fill our hearts with anything else will only leave us broken and hurting in the end.

What are some things people pursue other than healthy relationships with others?

Why do we pursue such things instead of healthy relationships?

Let's look at some relational counterfeits that vie for our hearts and attention:

- **Consumerism—commercials, social media, and celebrities tell us that buying certain products will make us happy and fulfill us.**

- **Busyness—smart phones, social media, streaming services, and gaming allow us to never be bored. But why must we be so busy all the time? Perhaps we are avoiding dealing with serious emotional hurts that distractions help us to keep at bay.**

- **Pornography—porn is an epidemic today. For many young people, looking at porn can be a way of avoiding the risk of real relationships.**

- **Social media—social media can be a great way to share ideas and connect with others. But social media connections can never replace the need for healthy, physical affection.**

- **Video games—video games can be a great source of entertainment and** community, but virtual accomplishments cannot replace meaning and significance in the real world.

What are some other ways that these things seem to offer meaning and value, but ultimately disappoint us?

How do healthy relationships ultimately fulfill what relational counterfeits merely promise to provide us?

It isn't enough to discuss why healthy relationships are important, though. We need to learn how to form healthy relationships.

What are some practical ways to develop healthy relationships?

One way is through finding common ground. Our closest friends were once complete strangers, but there was something about these people that connected us to them. To form relationships, we need to find things that we have in common and build upon them. Once we start doing that, we may find that we have even more in common than we had initially thought.

Another way to develop healthy relationships is by being a good listener. James 1:19 says to "be quick to hear, slow to speak." If we want others to hear us, we need to hear them as well. Being a good listener tells others that they are important to you. But listening is more than hearing. Before responding, try to genuinely understand what the other person is telling you.

The most famous friendship in the Bible is probably that of David and Jonathan. Let's look at the beginning of their friendship.

> **Read 1 Samuel 18:1-4 (NIV).**

After David had finished talking with Saul, Jonathan became one in spirit with David, and he loved him as himself. From that day Saul kept David with him and did not let him return home to his family. And Jonathan made a covenant with David because he loved him as himself. Jonathan took off the robe he was wearing and gave it to David, along with his tunic, and even his sword, his bow and his belt.

How did Jonathan show his friendship for David?

In these four verses, it is mentioned twice that Jonathan loved David as himself. This is also how Jesus taught us to love others (Matt. 22:39). A relationship is not a competition—seeking to gain importance over the other—but a genuine love and concern for the other's wellbeing. Also, Jonathan, son of the king, sacrificed of himself by giving his own belongings to David. Ultimately, he sacrificed more than his belongings for David. By being loyal to David, Jonathan cost himself the chance to be king of Israel. This is a great example of selfless love. True friends give sacrificially to one another, which also models how God loves us. John 3:16 says that God loved us so much that He gave us His only Son. God gave us His best and gave freely of Himself.

What are the problems affecting our society due to people not loving their neighbors?

Sadly, we see the effects in our society when people do not love or are not loved by others. There are many epidemics ravaging our society due, at least in part, to a lack of healthy relationships: loneliness, suicide, bullying, and racism. We will explore each of these issues during the week.

Provide some concrete ways we can address the following issues impacting our culture:

- **Loneliness**

- **Suicide**

- **Bullying**

- **Racism**

In this session, we have learned about the importance of maintaining healthy relationships. When they are lacking, we suffer not only as individuals, but also as a community and society. Over this week, let's make an intentional effort to form and to cultivate healthy relationships.

Day 1:
LONELINESS

Thanks to social media, you live in the most connected time in history. Yet, there is a mental health crisis looming for your generation, as loneliness has been on the rise for over a decade.[2]

How have you seen people struggle with loneliness?

Have you ever struggled with loneliness? If so, when do you feel most lonely?

What do you do to cope with loneliness?

When the pain of loneliness gets too deep, many teens act out to be noticed. This is exactly what happened to one of King David's sons, Absalom. Absalom murdered his brother, Amnon, out of revenge and fled to Geshur for three years. David finally agreed to allow Absalom to go back to Jerusalem, but David refused to see his son for another two years. Read what Absalom did to King David's military commander, Joab, to gain David's attention:

> **Read 2 Samuel 14:30-33.**

Then [Absalom] said to his servants, "See, Joab's field is next to mine, and he has barley there; go and set it on fire." So Absalom's servants set the field on fire. Then Joab arose and went to Absalom at his house and said to him, "Why have your servants set my field on fire?" Absalom answered Joab, "Behold, I sent word to you, 'Come here, that I may send you to the king, to ask, "Why have I come from Geshur? It would be better for me to be there still." Now therefore let me go into the presence of the king, and if there is guilt in me, let him put me to death.'" Then Joab went to the king and told him, and he [David] summoned Absalom. So he came to the king and bowed himself on his face to the ground before the king, and the king kissed Absalom.

What did Absalom do to get his father's attention?

What are some things that people do today to get attention?

Have you ever felt the pressure to act out in bizarre ways just to be seen? Just look at social media and the bizarre things people share for attention. Underneath, many of these reflect a heart cry for attention. This reveals the fact that human beings have been designed for relationship with God and other people. Our most important task is to lovingly relate to God and lovingly relate to other people. That's our purpose. That's why God created us. Life is about relationships.

How can you reach out to someone lonely today and relate to them in a loving way?

Day 2:
SUICIDE

We have all been affected by suicide. A friend. Family member. Classmate. Neighbor. Movie stars, athletes, and pastors. Maybe even you have considered it. Sadly, suicide is an epidemic today.

What are the reasons why people commit suicide?

Why would someone take their own life? There can be many contributing factors: bullying, failure, shame, loss, anger, revenge, loneliness, disappointment, substance abuse, broken relationships, hopelessness, and the list goes on. People who are suicidal are asking—whether they fully realize it or not—deep questions such as: Does my life have any meaning? Can I be forgiven? Am I loved? Is there any hope beyond my current pain?

How would you respond to someone asking these questions?

Suicide rates have risen at the same time as Christian influences have declined in our culture. Many today live with a naturalistic worldview, believing God does not exist and that everything can be explained by physical forces. If God does not exist and He is a delusion, then humans have no real value, death is the end, and life has no purpose. This is a hopeless worldview.

What are some things you can do in your everyday life to reveal to others the hope you have in Jesus?

Compared to naturalism, Christianity offers real hope. Jesus offers forgiveness, purpose, and genuine community. Jesus offers meaning in this life and hope for the next. Even if you don't feel like it, you are made in the image of God and have infinite worth. The worldview clash between naturalism and Christianity could not be starker.

How does Christianity answer the questions raised below?

Does my life have any meaning (John 10:9-10)?

Can I be forgiven (Eph. 1:7)?

Am I loved (John 3:16; Rom. 5:8)?

Is there any hope beyond my current pain (1 Thess. 4:13-14)?

WHAT CAN WE DO TO ADDRESS THE PROBLEM OF SUICIDE?

1. If you are having suicidal thoughts, you are not alone. When we are hurting, it is natural to feel like we are all alone or that no one understands. But this is not true. Many young people today struggle with suicidal thoughts. Please don't buy the lie that you are alone.

2. If you are having suicidal thoughts, talk with someone. Share your hurt with someone or call the suicide prevention hotline: (800) 273-8255. Please don't bury your hurt inside. If you get help, things can get better.

3. Look to help others who are hurting. People often give signs that they are having suicidal thoughts. If you see hear someone talking about ending their life, take it seriously. You could make the difference between life or death.

Day 3:
BULLYING

Studies show that roughly one in five students have been bullied.[3] If you have a class of a hundred students, that means roughly twenty have been bullied. That's a significant number. As Christians, since Jesus called us to leave the ninety-nine sheep and find the one, we should care if it were just one.

How would you define bullying?

Have you ever been bullied or witnessed someone else being bullied? If so, how did you respond?

What do you think drives bullies to act the way they do?

Researchers define bullying as unwanted, repeated aggressive behavior between two people with a power imbalance.[4] Essentially, a bully tries to make himself (or herself) feel better by putting another person down.

The Bible does not use the word "bullying," but it does directly and clearly address the actions inherent in bullying in the instructions it offers.

> **Read Mark 12:31.**

You shall love your neighbor as yourself.

What does it mean to love your neighbor as yourself?

How should this inform the way we interact with others?

Love involves sacrificing power for the well-being of another. Love is others centered. Bullying involves using power for selfish gain. Bullying is self-centered.

Read James 1:27.

Religion that is pure and undefiled before God the Father is this: to visit orphans and widows in their affliction, and to keep oneself unstained from the world.

What is the similarity between orphans and widows?

How does this apply to the issue of bullying?

As Christians, we are called to care about justice and to defend the oppressed. Jesus cared for the marginalized—women, children, the sick, the poor, and those who were demon-possessed. Why care about "lowly" people who were frequently rejected by society? Because every human being is made in the image of God and deserves dignity, honor, and respect (Gen. 1:28).

If Jesus were physically present today, He would stand up to bullies, have compassion on those who are bullied, and would never be a bystander. Since we are His followers, we must do what He would do.

Day 4:
RACISM

If we are going to love our neighbors from different ethnic backgrounds, we must be willing to truthfully assess our hearts regarding race. We must each be vulnerable, honest, and willing to consider our blind spots. We must commit to being part of the solution, not the problem.

There are three clear teachings to consider as we think biblically about racism.

> **Read Genesis 1:27-28a.**

So God created man in his own image, in the image of God he created him; male and female he created them. And God blessed them. And God said to them, "Be fruitful and multiply and fill the earth and subdue it."

> **What does this teach us about our relationship with people of different ethnicities?**

> **What about the way God created the world can teach us about His value of diversity?**

Scripture begins with the creation of the first couple, Adam and Eve, who become the parents of everyone. This means that all human beings, regardless of ethnicity, national boundary, or skin color are made in the image of God and reflect their Creator.

> **Look up in your Bible and read Acts 2:5-11.**

What do these verses teach us about God's value of diversity that we can apply to today?

On the day of Pentecost, which marks the beginning of the church, the Holy Spirit enabled the gospel to be understood by people from different countries and people groups. Why? Because the church is meant for young and old, male and female, and all races of people. Jesus gave His life for all people.

Read Revelation 7:9.

After this I looked, and behold, a great multitude that no one could number, from every nation, from all tribes and peoples and languages, standing before the throne and before the Lamb, clothed in white robes, with palm branches in their hands.

What does this teach us about God's value of diversity in the future?

John described a future consisting of a great multitude of people standing before God's throne "from every nation, from all tribes and peoples and languages." Heaven will be a beautifully diverse place.

If God so values diversity in the past, present, and future, then we also should reject anything that devalues others.

Session 3

Sex

WATCH ▬▬▬▬▬▬▬▬▬

**Use the fill-in-the-blanks and note-taking space as you watch the Session 3
teaching video together as a group.**

If the _____ is going to be _____ _____
with the created...

...there's going to have to be a point where we don't understand and yet

_____ _____ _____ _____.

The question is: Are we going to _____ _____ even if it doesn't make sense?

Why trust God? Because _____ _____ _____ (Ps. 19:7a; Deut. 10:12-13).

How would the world be if everybody lived out the sexual _____ _____

_____?

_____ sexually transmitted diseases

_____ crude sexual humor

_____ sexual abuse or sex trafficking

_____ divorce

_____ pornography

_____ abortion

_____ deadbeat dads

_____ same-sex marriage

Teaching videos are available at lifeway.com/thinkbiblically

GROUP DISCUSSION

The landscape for what is sexually acceptable in our culture is different today than in previous generations. In the "sexual revolution" of the 1960s, it was counter-cultural to have sex before marriage, to watch pornography, or to enter into an LGBTQ relationship. Today, these things are common. For many in our modern culture, God's design for marriage being the union of one man and one woman for one lifetime seems outdated, and maybe even bigoted.

Why do you think this is the case? Is this just the normal progression of society, or do you think there are other contributing factors?

Because you are growing up in such a sex-saturated culture, you have more hurdles to overcome to follow Jesus than any generation in modern history. You can hardly browse the internet, watch YouTube, enter social media, or walk down the street without getting bombarded with a counterfeit message about sex.

How many times a day do you think you are you presented messages about sex? Where does this happen most frequently?

In such a sex-saturated world, who can possibly expect you to follow God's design for relationships? The answer is simple: God does. His standards haven't changed, even if the world's have. You face incredible challenges in this arena, but you are capable of doing the right thing. God will "equip you with everything good that you may do his will" (Heb. 13:21).

> **Read Genesis 2:15-17 (NIV).**

The LORD God took the man and put him in the Garden of Eden to work it and take care of it. And the LORD God commanded the man, "You are free to eat from any tree in the garden; but you must not eat from the tree of the knowledge of good and evil, for when you eat from it you will certainly die."

Why do you think God gave the specific command not to eat of the fruit of the tree of the knowledge of good and evil?

Why didn't God give Adam a command like, "You can do anything in the garden, but don't murder Eve"?

Murdering someone is much worse than eating a piece of fruit, right? The difference is obeying a law against murder doesn't require trust. It's obvious that we shouldn't kill people. God created us to be in relationship with one another and with Him. Since He is our Creator, we are going to have to trust Him even when on the surface His instructions don't make sense.

What rules did your parents give you as a child that you didn't understand then, but that you understand better now?

In the garden of Eden, Satan tempted Adam and Eve by undermining their confidence in God's character. He appealed to their ambition for independence from God, eroded their trust in His goodness, and convinced them to do the one thing God commanded them not to do.

What are ways Satan does the same things to us today?

Today, Satan offers sex as "fruit" that looks pleasurable, fun, and satisfying. It is as if he were saying, "Is sexual activity really that big of a deal? Does porn really hurt anyone? As long as sex is consensual, there's nothing wrong with it, right? Why embrace a view of sex, love, and gender that seems so closed-minded? Isn't the Christian sexual ethic unrealistic today anyway?"

When there are so many messages contrary to God's Word, why should we trust God?

The biggest reason to trust God is because of Jesus. Jesus reveals God's character through His tender kindness, His compassion, and His willingness to die so that we might have life. If you want to know what God is like, look at Jesus. Jesus is the all-knowing, self-existing God in human flesh. And He lived the most loving, gracious, and beautiful life ever.

Not only is God good, but His commands are for our good. We may not understand all of God's commandments about sex, but the biggest question is: Will we trust Him?

What would the world be like if everyone lived the sexual ethic of Jesus, prescribed in the Bible?

Here are some examples:

- There would be no sexual exploitation, sexual trafficking, or sexual abuse.
- There would be no sexually transmitted diseases.
- There would be no pain from divorce.
- Kids would be brought into a family with a mom and dad who love each other.

Wouldn't such a world be far better than our own? The answer is obvious.

Do you think God's design offers more freedom or less freedom? Defend your answer.

Sex in marriage means you are free to enjoy sex without fear of negative consequences. Following God's plan for sex enables couples to not worry about rejection, comparison, contracting an STD, or any other unforeseen consequence of sex outside of marriage. They are free to experience intimacy within a relationship built on trust and commitment. Simply put, God's plans are not meant to steal our fun, but to help us flourish in our relationships with our spouse.

Yet, many young people today think they are free to do whatever they want sexually as long as there is consent and no one gets hurt.

What do you think about this?

This is not true freedom. Real freedom is having the capacity to live as God designed you regardless of how you feel. We only experience real freedom when we follow the loving plan of our Creator who knows us best and designed us with purpose.

What is God's design for sex?

Of course, sex is pleasurable. God designed it that way! It's perfectly fine for a married couple to enjoy sex. But let's explore it more deeply. The Bible gives three main purposes for sex:

1. **Procreation:** Simply put, sex is how babies are made. Being fruitful and multiplying on the earth is both a command and a blessing (Gen. 1:28).

2. **Unity:** One of the most powerful aspects of sex is its ability to bond people together. Genesis 2:24 says, "Therefore a man shall leave his father and his mother and hold fast to his wife, and they shall become one flesh." When a couple has sex, something changes in their relationship. They have entered into a deeper "one flesh" union that is not only spiritual, but also emotional, relational, and even biochemical (which is one reason it is especially difficult for teenagers to break up after they have been sexually active).

3. **Foreshadow heaven:** Sex is beautiful. But remember, it is merely a foreshadowing of the deep intimacy we will experience with God and others in heaven. Sexual union on earth is a foreshadowing of the deeper union we will all experience in heaven, the experience of being known without shame.

When people focus merely on the physical element of sex, and ignore the relational, spiritual, and emotional dimensions, they miss the deeper unity—the intimate connection—that occurs between two people in the act of sex. Since our culture has lost the deeper meaning of sex, and focuses merely on the physical, many people today think that sex itself is the route to happiness. Our culture desperately misses the fact that even the most wonderful sex life cannot satisfy the craving of the human heart for love and connection.

How has this discussion changed your view of sex?

WHAT ARE SOME WAYS WE CAN EXPERIENCE GOD'S GOOD DESIGN FOR SEX?

- **First, avoid sexually tempting situations.** Whether it is avoiding parties, certain social media apps, or being on your phone when you are alone, the wise Christian thinks about sexually tempting situations ahead of time and avoids them.

- **Second, have an accountability structure.** Whether it's a parent, youth pastor, teacher or friend, we all need someone to ask us the tough questions about our sexual choices, to show us grace when we fail, and to help keep us accountable.

- **Third, experience God's grace.** No matter what you have done, or has been done to you, God forgives you and can restore you from the pain you may have experienced. He yearns for you to experience His love, forgiveness, and restoration. Don't let your past determine your future. God loves you and is for you.

Day 1:
HOMOSEXUALITY

As an atheist with same-sex attraction, Rachel never thought she would end up becoming a follower of Jesus. But it happened. God began to change her life radically, but some nagging questions persisted. Let's see how you might respond to her questions:

What should I do with my same-sex attraction?

Why would God not want me to act on my attractions?

If it felt so right to be attracted to the same sex, how could it be condemned as wrong?

Rachel understood what the Bible teaches about same-sex unions, but she struggled to understand why. As she wrestled with the issue, the most pressing question in her mind became, "Will I obey God, even if I don't understand?"

Why should we follow commands from God even if we don't understand them?

There is one good reason: Trust in the one who gave it. Rachel ultimately decided that God could be trusted with her sexuality.

Now, let's address a very important question: Can you be gay and Christian? The answer depends on what is meant by "gay." Let's consider three different ways this question can be taken.

Can a Christian experience same-sex attraction?

Of course. Same-sex attraction doesn't magically disappear when someone chooses to follow Jesus.

Can a Christian commit sexual sin, including same-sex behavior, and be forgiven?

Absolutely! The Bible takes same-sex sexual behavior seriously, as it does all forms of sexual sin, but the Bible also says, "If we confess our sins, he is faithful and just to forgive us our sins and to cleanse us from all unrighteousness" (1 John 1:9).

Can a person engage in unrepentant same-sex behavior and be a Christian?

The key word in the question is "unrepentant." Christians will struggle with sin their entire lives, but a committed follower of Christ does not desire to continue in any lifestyle contrary to God's design and commands. The desire of a Christian is to obey Jesus and follow His teachings. That means a Christian should live in a way that honors God in how they think about and practice sexual activity.

HOW SHOULD WE RESPOND TO A PERSON WHO STRUGGLES WITH SAME-SEX ATTRACTION?

1. **If you are a Christian who experiences same-sex attraction, please know that you are not alone.** There are many Christians, young and old, who understand. You are not a mistake or broken beyond God's grace. God loves you deeply.

2. **Be a good friend.** How can you be the type of friend that loves others with the love of Jesus?

3. **Stay faithful to Scripture.** True freedom comes not from rejecting the teachings of Jesus, but from trusting our lives to the one who made us and loves us.

Day 2:
TRANSGENDER

While the Bible is the best-selling book of all time, *Harry Potter* the best-selling book series.[1] The author, J.K. Rowling, has been one of the most beloved authors on the planet for decades, but recently all that began to change. People have accused her of hatred, called her vile names, and threatened her because she challenged the transgender narrative.[2]

Rowling became concerned about certain groups of people who were experiencing negative effects because of trans-activism. She was also deeply troubled by the massive increase in young girls who are being referred to transitioning treatment.

Why do you think there are so many young people—especially girls—who identify as transgender today?

In her book *Irreversible Damage: The Transgender Craze Seducing Our Daughters*, Abigail Shrier explores the question of why there has been such an increase in young people—and especially adolescent girls—identifying as transgender. "We should begin" she says, "by noting that adolescent girls today are in a lot of pain."[3]

What are the various pains that young girls often feel today?

Depression. Loneliness. Anxiety. Suicide. As we explored in earlier chapters, these phenomena have been rising among young people.

Why do you think this is the case?

How do you think this relates to the growth of people claiming transgender identities?

According to Shrier, a transgender identity promises freedom from anxiety, satisfies the need for belonging, and offers the thrill of rebellion.[4] Identifying as transgender is one way some young people aim to fulfill the deep human needs that we all share. Of course, this is not the only reason someone identifies as transgender. But there is far more to the story than you may typically hear.

Regardless of what the culture may say, we must always remember God's initial design for humanity:

Read Genesis 1:27.

So God created man in his own image,
in the image of God he created him;
male and female he created them.

We are naturally born as male or female by God's design from the very beginning, which Jesus reinforced in the New Testament (Matt. 19:4).

WHAT CAN WE DO TO HELP OUR TRANSGENDER FRIENDS?

1. **Love them.** Your transgender friends want love, belonging, happiness, and the same things all of us want.

2. **Be quick to listen and slow to speak.** James, the half-brother of Jesus said to be "quick to hear, slow to speak" (James 1:19). Rather than look to "fix" people who are transgender, focus on being a good listener.

3. **Speak truth compassionately.** Be willing to speak truth and do so with kindness. Like the apostles of Jesus, be more concerned with obeying God than satisfying than the opinions of people (Acts 4:18-20; 5:29). Only the truth can set people free.

Day 3:
PORNOGRAPHY

Every generation has faced sexual temptation, but compared with the history of the world, there are some radical shifts that have taken place in your generation. Pornography has drastically transformed how people think about sex, love, dating, and relationships.

Do you think porn is a big deal? Why or why not?

What are ways that porn harms us?

You might be tempted to think that porn doesn't affect you. The data shows that it harms you in three ways:

1. **Porn harms your soul.** Young people who look at porn are more likely to be sexually aggressive, have more permissive sexual attitudes, accept the notion of casual sex, engage in risky sexual behavior, engage in sexual harassment and suffer with depression.[5]

2. **Porn harms your beliefs.** Porn offers an unrealistic, exaggerated, and harmful script for sex. Porn portrays marital sex as boring, but extramarital sex as exciting. It presents people not as individuals to be loved and cherished, but as sex objects to be used by others for pleasure. Violent porn sends the message that people can be harmed if others enjoy it.

3. **Porn harms your brain.** Few people realize how deeply porn rewires the brain and shapes human behavior. Research shows that porn is far harder to quit than gambling, alcohol addiction, heroin, and cocaine because of what porn does to your brain.[6]

WHAT CAN WE DO TO AVOID THE SNARE OF PORNOGRAPHY?

- **If you struggle with porn, I urge you to talk with someone you know who cares.** Please don't allow shame or fear of what others may think to keep you from getting help. Satan uses those feelings to keep us mired in our sin. Plus, far more people struggle with pornography than you may realize. You are not alone.

- **Remember that God loves you.** If you struggle with porn, God wants you to experience His love and forgiveness. Confess your sin to God and believe that He loves you deeply and can help you (Luke 15:11-32).

- **Realize that porn use often masks a deeper brokenness.** Pornography aims to fill the good desire God has given us with a "relational counterfeit." Addressing habitual porn use must begin with the goal of becoming relationally healthy through building intimate connections with God and other people.

- **Consider asking how you can make a difference.** Share this chapter with a friend. Post a video critical of porn on social media.[7] Give a talk in school on the harm of pornography. Or, simply be there for someone struggling with porn— not to judge, but simply to show grace, love, support, and accountability. You can make a difference.

Day 4:
ABORTION

In June 2022, the Supreme Court overturned Roe v. Wade. This decision made the "right" to abortion a state issue rather than a federal one. States can now have different laws.[8] Thus, making a case for life as vital as ever.

There have been tens of millions of abortions in the United States over the past few decades. Many more people than you can imagine have had an experience with abortion, probably even someone you know personally.

What are the reasons why women have abortions?

As we aim to consider each topic in this study with grace and truth, let's remember: this issue involves every one of us. God values all life from the womb until death. We should have the same attitude.

How would you make a case against abortion?

The science is clear: at fertilization, the unborn is a living, individual human being separate from the mother. Yet, some pro-choice advocates point to differences between those in the womb and those outside the womb to deny the unborn the right to life. There are four key differences (which spell "SLED") but none of these are significant enough to deny the right to life of the unborn. They are Size, Level of Development, Environment, and Degree of Dependency.[9]

S-Size: Does size have anything to do with the right to life? Is a basketball player more valuable than a gymnast? Just because the fetus is smaller than an adult does not mean it is not a valuable human being.

L-Level of Development: The unborn are less developed than newborns and adults. But this has no relevance to its essential nature as a human being. Are adults more valuable than elementary children because they have gone through puberty? Are people with mental and physical disabilities less valuable because their brains and bodies developed differently? Human development (and thus, value) begins at fertilization and continues throughout life.

E-Environment: Unborn humans live in a different location than newborns and adults, but why is that relevant to its value? Do you stop being human when you change your location? How can where you are determine what you are?

D-Degree of Dependency: The unborn is fully dependent upon its mother for survival. Why does this make it a less valuable human being? If your humanity hinged upon how dependent you were, then what about toddlers, the handicapped, and those on dialysis machines?

Give an example for each of the four differences to show why it fails to determine the value of a human being:

- **Size-**

- **Level of Development-**

- **Environment-**

- **Degree of Dependency-**

What can you do to make an impact for life?

Here are some other ways to make an impact for life: Share the SLED argument with a friend. Make a social media post defending life. Visit a pregnancy resource center. Support pro-life causes.

Here's the bottom line: The unborn cannot speak up for themselves. Will you speak up for them?

We must also remember in this issue, no one ever changed their minds because someone yelled at them or called them awful names. Changed hearts only come through love—both ours and the Lord's— and genuine relationships.

Session 4

Care

WATCH

Use the fill-in-the-blanks and note-taking space as you watch the Session 4 teaching video together as a group.

We can approach every issue_____, and if we do it with

___ _____ _____ toward others, it's amazing how much _____

_____ _____.

How do we approach an issue like climate change biblically?

Step 1: Go to the _____ (Acts 17:11).

Creation is _____ .

Step 2: _____ _____ calls us to _____ ____ _____ (Gen. 1:28, NIV).

Show humility (Prov. 11:2).

Step 3: Examine _____ sides (Prov. 18:17, CSB).

The first to state his case seems right until another comes and cross-examines him.

When it comes to climate change:

Avoid _____ _____.

Avoid _____ _____.

Let's think _____ about _____.

Teaching videos are available at lifeway.com/thinkbiblically

GROUP DISCUSSION

Imagine you're in a class discussing a hot-button social or political issue, say gun control or climate change. Maybe you stayed silent, not knowing what to say. Maybe you argued for a position you believe in. Maybe you won. Maybe you lost. Maybe it was a draw. If you reflect for a moment, where did your beliefs come from? Your parents? YouTube videos? Honestly, how confident are you that your beliefs are true? Have you really considered opposing views? What if you're wrong?

Where do you think most of your beliefs have come from?

How much time and effort do you put into researching views different than yours?

One of the challenges of growing up today is that you're expected to have an opinion on everything. Because of the reach of social media, it seems like we are all expected to speak to a range of issues. In fact, sometimes we are criticized for not speaking up!

Was there a time or an issue about which you felt pressured to comment, even if you weren't positive about your position? If so, what was it and what happened?

In our honest moments, we all wonder if we really know what we're talking about. Do we speak up because we really believe in an issue, or because we want our friends to think we're good, informed, articulate people?

When do you feel most inclined to speak on an issue, when you have strong convictions about it or when it's a popular topic of discussion among your friends?

Before we go any further, I want to relieve you of something: You don't have to have an opinion on everything. It's okay to say, "I don't know." In fact, it can be virtuous to withhold having an opinion on something while you gain more information! James 1:19 says to be quick to hear and slow to speak. I would encourage you to focus on asking more questions, and aiming to understand, rather than feeling the need to have an opinion on everything.

When have you wished you had spoken up on a particular issue?

When have you wished you had stayed silent?

Maybe you feel like you aren't informed enough on the important issues. Maybe you feel like you're still too young to have an opinion or a voice. Don't let anyone look down on you because you are young. Your opinion does matter. You can think through pressing issues today and make a difference.

Read 1 Timothy 4:12 (NIV).

Don't let anyone look down on you because you are young, but set an example for the believers in speech, in conduct, in love, in faith and in purity.

What do you think about the first eleven words in this verse?

Why is the second half of Paul's command so important for us today?

Just because you are young, it does not mean you can't influence your family and friends. It may not even be due to your vast knowledge, but simply because you are loving and respectful. Being loving and respectful in how you express your opinion is key. This verse doesn't give you permission to be a "know it all" or insert yourself in every conversation and situation. It just gives you permission to lovingly and respectfully have an informed opinion and express it in discussions without feeling inadequate or insecure. Showing thought and care in your words will make it more likely for others to consider your thoughts on an issue.

What are some practical ways we can model love and grace in our everyday conversations, as well as when discussing controversial issues with others?

Besides knowing how to model love and respect in our conversations, it is also important to understand the issues. Now, the Bible does not specifically address most issues in this study. Quite obviously, there's no passage in the Bible that discusses gun control. Even on the issue of poverty, which the Bible discusses regularly, there are big cultural differences between biblical times and today. The Bible doesn't specifically answer, for instance, whether or not we should give to people who hold signs by the side of the road.

How can we approach issues the Bible does not speak to directly?

Here are a few steps that will help:

1. **Gather the facts.** Don't rely on headlines and hot takes when searching for truth. Many headlines are simply click-bait and meant to grab people's attention and to get views. Read entire articles. Check out sources and footnotes. Also, make sure you consider both sides of an issue. Proverbs 18:17 (NIV) says, "In a lawsuit the first to speak seems right, until someone comes forward and cross-examines." The view opposite of what you hold may have some good arguments that you need to address. It may even be correct. Don't stop searching when you find an answer that you like. Keep going until you are confident you have the truth, even if that truth is uncomfortable.

   When was the last time you changed your mind on an issue? What caused that to happen?

2. **Find biblical principles that relate to the current issue.** For instance, the Bible does not discuss climate change, but it does talk about the environment by calling us to care for creation (Gen. 1:28-29). Therefore, we shouldn't pollute or litter. We should care about the earth and the animals that God created. We must think about the environmental impact of our decisions since the planet is our home and God's gift to us. Since we share the earth with everyone else, caring for creation is also a way of loving our neighbors. Of course, this does not even scratch the surface of the climate change debate, but it's a start. Scripture doesn't directly address many issues we deal with today, but it provides stories and teachings that can help us approach them wisely.

   What biblical teaching—while maybe not tying directly to immigration, gun control, or another current issue—can help guide us on all issues?

3. **Be loving toward non-Christians who come to different conclusions.** They hold different views because they have a different worldview, which likely includes not believing in the authority of Scripture. On your part, don't let a difference on an ethical issue break your relationship with that person (Rom. 12:18). Remember, the biggest goal is that the person comes to know Jesus, not that you win an argument.

What can you do to maintain friendships with non-Christians who may hold radically different views on important cultural issues?

Even with fellow Christians, we want to show love and respect to those who come to different conclusions (which doesn't include life, marriage, deity of Jesus, etc.). For example, the Bible tells us we must provide for the poor. But we may disagree on whether it is best done on the personal level, through community-based charities, or by government programs. In the same way, Christians also disagree on secondary theological issues, such as spiritual gifts and the age of the earth. But Christians cannot differ on the essentials, such as the divinity of Jesus, salvation by grace, and the bodily resurrection of Jesus.[1]

Throughout the week, pay attention to the way you discuss important social and political issues. Are you arguing with love and grace, or simply to win a fight? Also, think about the ways you form your opinions on important matters. Do you simply go along with what your friends and family say, or have you conducted your own research? When presented with a new issue, is your first inclination to search the internet or the Scriptures? As you grow in this practice, you will also grow in your ability to set an example for other believers.

Day 1:
CLIMATE CHANGE

Sea levels are rising. Polar bears are dying. Air is becoming increasingly polluted. Floods, fires, droughts, and storms are increasing at unprecedented rates. If we don't make drastic changes in our approach to the climate, billions of people will die and civilization will likely end within a decade.

How often do you hear statements like these?

How much does this concern you?

Many in your generation cite climate changes as the most important issue facing the world today.[2] Therefore, we must think about it carefully and biblically. So, let's avoid two extremes:

1. **Climate Alarmism-** Climate alarmism is not new. A few decades ago, there were reports that the world was entering another ice age. Now they're talking about global warming! Don't believe climate alarmists. The world is not ending soon because of climate change.

2. **Climate Change Denial-** The opposite extreme is climate change denial. There is no debate that Earth's climate has naturally changed throughout its history and sometimes dramatically. Scientists are increasingly confident that climate change occurs today and humans are playing a role. The important concerns are the amount humans contribute to climate change and what to do about it.

What is our responsibility toward taking care of the planet?

Read Genesis 1:28.

God blessed them and said to them, "Be fruitful and increase in number; fill the earth and subdue it. Rule over the fish in the sea and the birds in the sky and over every living creature that moves on the ground."

What does this verse mean? How would you rephrase it in your own words?

God put humans in charge of "stewarding" creation—which means to take care of it. Stewardship involves enjoying God's creation, but also protecting, preserving, and ruling over what God has made. It involves harvesting crops, building roads for transportation, cutting down trees to make homes, and making things like clothes and smartphones. One way we love God is by caring for His beautiful creation. We honor God and love our neighbors by protecting the environment that we all inhabit.

WHAT CAN WE DO IN RESPONSE TO THE CLIMATE CHANGE DEBATE?

1. **Don't be taken by bad ideas or bad science.** Examine both sides, ask deep questions, and follow the truth wherever it leads.

2. **Care for the environment in obedience to God.** Even small things, like picking up trash, are ways to love your neighbor.

3. **Consider a life profession that aims to care for creation.**

Day 2:
POVERTY

A few years ago, my friend Dan called me and asked if we could meet for coffee. He was leaving his comfortable pastoral position at a beach community in Southern California to work at the Urban Rescue Mission in Los Angeles, which is in the heart of Skid Row.

Why would someone make such a decision?

The simple answer is that God started to change his heart. When Dan studied the scriptural command to care for the poor, he became increasingly uncomfortable regarding his comfortable life.

What does Scripture say about caring for the poor? Write down everything you can think of.

Now, compare your list with these ten biblical commands.

1. **Make provision for the poor (Lev. 19:9-10).**

2. **Treat the poor justly (Lev. 19:15).**

3. **Help the poor (Lev. 25:35-36).**

4. **Defend the rights of the poor (Ps. 82:3-4).**

5. **Be generous to the poor (Prov. 14:21).**

6. **Do not oppress the poor (Prov. 14:31).**

7. Hear the cries of the poor (Prov. 21:13).

8. Serve the poor and treat them with honor (Luke 14:12-14).

9. Do not discriminate against the poor (Jas. 2:2-4).

10. Remember the poor (Gal. 2:10).

After reviewing these verses, why is it important to help the poor?

Ultimately, poverty stems not just from a lack of money or things but from broken relationships with God, others, and self. If we want to address poverty, we must be willing to give and to help people cultivate a proper understanding of their own worth and develop healthy relationships with God and others. When people have healthy relationships, they are in a better position to experience the dignity that comes from working and supporting themselves and their families.

HOW CAN YOU HELP THOSE IN POVERTY?

1. **Don't buy the lie that the purpose of life is to get things.** This pursuit leads to emptiness. A "rich" life is one that consists of meaningful relationships with God and other people that is focused on building God's kingdom.

2. **Be grateful for what you have.** You probably have more to be thankful for than you realize. You most likely have adults who care about you, a roof over your head, and your basic needs met. Have you ever thanked God for these things?

3. **Be generous with others.** Even if you are young and may not have a lot of money, give what you can. We must be good stewards of everything God has given us, especially money and resources. Plus, anything can make a difference, no matter how great or small.

Day 3:
GUN CONTROL

Your generation has been deeply shaped by the reality of gun violence. Movies, song lyrics, social media, and video games often glorify violence. Firearm-related injuries are among the leading causes of death among teens.[3] Sadly, we are all too familiar with school shootings. There have even been shootings in churches and places of worship in recent years.

So let's step back from some of the emotion surrounding this issue and try to think clearly about God and guns.

Is it ever okay for a follower of Jesus to take another person's life? If so, when?

How do I balance the command to love my enemies with the right to self-defense in emergency situations?

Most of the modern debate about gun ownership is not if people should be able to own them, but what kinds of weapons people should be able to own and under what conditions can they can carry them.

What is your view on gun control?

Some Christians are opposed to Christ followers ever taking the life of another human being. While violence clearly existed in Old Testament times, pacifists believe we should look to Jesus who willingly lay down His life for us as our example. Even more, He calls His followers to "pick up their crosses" and do the same for others (Mark 8:34).

In contrast to pacifism, many Christians believe they have a right to self-defense, including owning a gun, because they are pro-life. If a gun is necessary for self-defense, then owning a gun can be justified as a means of securing the right to protect life.

Which perspective do you agree with more, and why?

WHAT STEPS CAN WE TAKE IN THE GUN CONTROL DEBATE?

1. **If you own a gun, be careful to avoid idolatry.** The Bible gives caution against trusting weapons and violence. Psalm 44:6 says, "For not in my bow do I trust, nor can my sword save me."

2. **We should avoid naïve laws or mandates that overlook man's capacity for evil.** We need genuinely effective laws, not just good intentions.

3. **We should pursue effective laws that will actually help to restrain man's capacity for evil.** Any human being who uses a gun has a deeply fallen nature and is capable of great evil. Thus, it seems that every Christian should be committed to supporting laws that minimize the effects of human sinfulness and protect human lives.

We must ask ourselves: What is ultimately more important, our legal rights as citizens of the United States or loving God and others as citizens of the kingdom of heaven?

Day 4:
IMMIGRATION

As Christians, we must begin the immigration discussion with a recognition of the humanity of immigrants rather than the best policy regarding immigration. We must approach the conversation with a caring demeanor and a desire to love immigrants as people made in the image of God.

What is your stance on immigration? How has the Bible informed your views?

While there are considerable differences between biblical times and today, the Bible has a lot to say about how we should treat immigrants. Let's consider two big points.

POINT #1: GOD CARES FOR IMMIGRANTS

Consider how many key figures in the Bible were either immigrants or refugees:

- **Abraham sought refuge in Egypt to escape a famine (Gen. 12).**

- **Moses fled from Pharaoh to the land of Midian (Ex. 2).**

- **All of Jerusalem, except for the poorest people, became refugees and exiles when they were defeated and deported to Babylon (2 Kings 24).**

- **Joseph and Mary fled to Egypt during the slaughter of the children by Herod. They later moved to Nazareth (Matt. 2).**

The Bible is full of stories of immigrants and refugees. These immigrants are not shown to be a problem for God's plan, but instead God worked through them to further carry out His will.

Has this affected your view of immigration? Why or why not?

POINT #2: GOD COMMANDS HIS FOLLOWERS TO CARE FOR IMMIGRANTS

Scripture consistently demonstrates God's heart for outsiders. For instance, the people of Israel were commanded not to strip their vineyards bare, so sojourners and the poor could collect some for food (Lev. 19:10). Immigrants would receive part of the tithes so they could eat (Deut. 26:12). There were serious consequences for Israelites who took advantage of immigrants (Deut. 27:19).

Should people be allowed to move from country to country without any regulation?

God ordained governments to protect and care for its own citizens. Like a mother who cares for her kids, governments have an obligation to care for their citizens. Unauthorized immigration, for example, does raise legitimate national security concerns. Any nation is unwise to have light immigration policies that allow anyone through its borders without knowing who they are and where they come from.

How can you love an immigrant?

Is there someone at your school, in your community, or on a sports team that you can befriend? Listen to them. Hear their stories. Ask about their family. Be curious about their lives and what it's like in America. Learn from them. Try to treat them as you would want them to treat you if you were an immigrant. Don't tease them or act superior to them because they may look or act differently than everyone else. Isn't that what Jesus would do?

Session 5

Culture

WATCH

Use the fill-in-the-blanks and note-taking space as you watch the Session 5 teaching video together as a group.

What we see affects how we _____ and how we _____ (Rom. 12:2a).

Three ways social media and smart phones might affect us:

1. Smart phones and social media affect us_____.

"I keep myself busy to avoid the _____ in my heart."

2. Smart phones and social media can affect us _____.

3. Smart phones and social media affect our _____.

What might it look like to renew our minds with social media and smart phones?

Some things to keep in mind:

1. Have _____ (in terms of places and in terms of time).

2. Take _____ _____.

3. Follow _____ examples.

4. _____ about what you _____ and_____.

5. Talk with _____ _____about what you see.

6. Run it through_____.

Teaching videos are available at lifeway.com/thinkbiblically

GROUP DISCUSSION

What do you think affects you more, what you physically put into your body or what you allow into your mind?

What you eat has a huge impact on your body and mood, such as focus, weight, and so on. Drinking an energy drink will—you guessed it—give you a temporary boost of energy. Stuffing yourself like a Thanksgiving turkey may put you into a food coma, but what we watch also affects us. Companies spend millions on advertising knowing that the messages and images they present will encourage you to buy their product. Trends grow and explode on social media because people mimic what they see.

Have you ever taken part of a viral social media challenge or trend (Like the ALS ice bucket challenge or the "End It" campaign to eliminate sex slavery)? If so, what was it?

Be honest: Why did you do it? Was it because you thought the challenge or trend was interesting or worthwhile, or was it because everyone else was doing it?

The opening question was really a trick question. Since we are body and soul, physical and spiritual, both really matter, but in different ways. The apostle Paul certainly knew this.

> **Read Galatians 5:16-17.**

But I say, walk by the Spirit, and you will not gratify the desires of the flesh. For the desires of the flesh are against the Spirit, and the desires of the Spirit are against the flesh, for these are opposed to each other, to keep you from doing the things you want to do.

How do we avoid submitting to the desires of the flesh?

What does it mean to walk by the Spirit?

What are the spiritual disciplines that keep us walking by the Spirit?

Galatians 5:19-21 lists works of the flesh that will prevent us from inheriting the kingdom of God. One of them is drunkenness. Drugs and alcohol cause us to get enslaved to the body because they are so addictive. This is why Paul encouraged us to walk by the Spirit, so that we will not become enslaved by the desires of the flesh.

As mentioned earlier, our consumption is more than just the physical. We must also be mindful of what we consume mentally, through social media and entertainment. Now, these are both good things. I love my smartphone and I love movies, but social media and entertainment contain ideas that shape how we think about the world. They affect us both emotionally and intellectually. Therefore, Paul's command in 2 Corinthians 10:5 to "take every thought captive to obey Christ" is especially important to us in our world of constant messaging through the media.

> **What are some practical ways to live out 2 Corinthians 10:5, thinking specifically about what we consume as entertainment and what we view on social media?**

Which social media platform is your favorite, and why?

Did you know that popular social media apps are designed to be as addictive as drugs?[1] In fact, they trigger similar parts of the brain to release chemicals that feel good so you will want to stay on the app and come back to it for the same high.[2] Even though social media enters through the mind, unlike drugs in the body, they are both addictive. Social media designers want people to spend maximum time and money on their apps and are designed to cause addiction. Yet, again, we are to be led by the Spirit not the flesh.

How much time do you spend on social media every day?

Think about the reasons why you use social media. What are some other screenless activities that can fulfill the same purpose?

Some of the most significant messaging that has overtaken social media and entertainment in the recent years is political. In fact, it seems that everything in our culture is now politicized, from businesses to sports. Even if you aren't interested in politics at all, you are being presented political messaging everywhere you look.

What are the political messages you see most frequently, and where do you encounter them?

How do you respond to political messaging, especially ideas with which you disagree?

Since politics has invaded everything in our society, we need to know how to navigate the issues wisely.

Where do you learn about the news or things happening in the world, if at all? Social media? Traditional media?

Why do you trust this source?

What are the problems with getting news from both social media and traditional media?

We need to focus on what we allow into our minds. The news we see on social media can be accurate or it can be "click-bait." Maybe all your friends have the same political views, so you only get one side of every issue. After all, most people make up their minds because of what their friends or family believe. We need to make sure we examine all sides of every issue, that we are pursuing truth, and not simply reinforcing what we already believe.

How do we avoid being taken in by "click-bait" messaging?

How do we prevent becoming biased and only getting one side of an issue?

When thinking through an important issue, how much time do you spend finding a biblical perspective?

As Christians, we must always consider what the Bible has to say on the issues. We explored this in the last session, how not every issue has a clear-cut answer in Scripture. But we can always find a guiding principle if we dig deep enough.

As important as politics are, though, we need to keep our priorities straight. Our primary allegiance must not be to a political party, but to God and building His kingdom (Matt. 6:33). Earlier we discussed Paul's command to take our thoughts captive to Christ. Take note, in the previous two verses, Paul reminded us "though we live in the world, we do not wage war as the world does. The weapons we fight with are not the weapons of the world" (2 Cor. 10:3-4, NIV). This means even though we are constantly bombarded with political and social messaging, we must remember that the ultimate struggle in this world is not physical or even political, but spiritual.

How do we live out Matthew 6:33 and keep ourselves from being consumed by political or social issues?

Bottom line: We must be mindful of what we allow into our bodies, and we must also consider what we allow into our minds. The media we consume can impact our health just as much as anything we eat or drink. Ultimately, everything we do and think must be filtered through a biblical worldview.

Day 1:
SOCIAL MEDIA

I remember the first time I watched YouTube, searched Instagram for pictures of my friends, and sent a tweet. I also remember a world without any of these. My guess is that you probably experience the world through a different lens. After all, you were likely swiping a screen before you could even speak! Smartphones and social media have always been part of the world you grew up in.

What would the world be like without social media?

My generation may struggle to understand new digital technologies. And your generation, because you have no experience of a world without smartphones and social media, may struggle to see how deeply they affect you. Given that they've always been around, you may not have thought about them much at all!

How do you think social media shapes our lives? Think about how it affects you personally as well as how it affects the way you relate with others. Write down your thoughts, and then compare with the list below.

FIVE WAYS SOCIAL MEDIA AFFECTS OUR LIVES

1. **Social media affects how we assess truth.** Many social media platforms display data like the number of views or "likes" a post has. Popularity has nothing to do with if something is true or false. Be careful not to confuse number of views or "likes" with truth.

2. **Social media affects us emotionally.** Sometimes we use social media simply as a means to keep ourselves busy and distracted to avoid dealing with painful issues in our lives.

3. **Social media affects us spiritually.** Social media encourages the worldview of individualism—the idea that life is all about you. It encourages you to do whatever it takes to get followers and "likes" so you can be popular. The Bible teaches us life is not all about us.

4. **Social media affects our identities.** If a certain post gets "likes," we are tempted to do it more to increase our popularity. This encourages us to find value or claim our identity in what other people say about us rather than what God says in Scripture.

5. **Social media affects our relationships.** Social media encourages us to care more about crafting an impressive persona than making genuine friends. It also distracts us from being present when we are around others.

I'm not saying social media is completely bad. To be honest, I love my smartphone! The key is to be reflective about how it affects us and wise about how we use it.

WHAT ARE SOME HEALTHY GUIDELINES WHEN USING SOCIAL MEDIA?

1. **Think before posting a picture, video, or comment.**

2. **Take a break from social media and set limits.**

3. **Use technology for good.**

4. **Be positive.**

Day 2:
ENTERTAINMENT

Even though my family lives in Southern California, not far from the beach, my oldest son rarely goes in the water. And when he does, it's often not for long. Why? He's afraid of sharks even though he knows the chances of getting attacked are extremely low. I think his fear comes from the time I made the mistake of showing him *Jaws* when he was only eight. The movie has haunted him since. Yeah, that was a parenting fail. Though it may not be as obvious for us as it is my son, all of us are shaped more deeply than we even realize by the movies and television shows we watch.

Are there any movies or television shows that have affected your life in a profound way?

Do you have any guidelines for assessing entertainment?

Movies and TV shows can be an especially powerful means of persuasion because we often let down our guards when watching them. The point of a movie or TV show is to entertain us. Movies and TV certainly are entertaining, but can be much more than that. If we're not careful, we can allow ourselves to be influenced by the ideas and worldviews embedded within them.

In assessing movies and TV shows, it is important that we consider how violence, sex, and vulgar language are portrayed. Does the movie praise violence? Does it portray sex outside of marriage as cool? Or does it show the consequences of certain behavior and discourage immorality?

Interestingly, the Bible contains all sorts of sex, violence, and immoral behavior.

Why do you think the Bible contains content like this?

The Bible does not include these stories in an exploitive fashion, but to show that sin has consequences. The immoral behavior in the Bible is not meant to attract us, but to appall us. The Bible uses physical and graphic violence to teach a moral lesson about the horrors of sin so we will avoid it.

We previously defined a worldview as "view of the world." But a worldview is also a story that answers three key questions:

- **How did we get here (origin)?**

- **What went wrong (predicament)?**

- **How do we fix it (resolution)?**

  How do movies and TV shows follow the same basic structure?

Every movie and TV show has these three acts. The reason worldviews, TV shows, and movies are so similar is because they are stories. Christianity is a story about reality. Buddhism is a story about reality. Atheism is a story about reality. And every movie is a story about reality.

While every story says something about reality, not every story accurately reflects reality. This is why we must think biblically about them. We must learn to filter ideas in movies through a biblical lens.

Day 3:
POLITICS

You may not be old enough to vote, so you might be wondering why there is a session on politics in this study. Even if you can't vote yet, you are affected by politics and likely have some political views you've already formed.

At what age or stage of life do you think people should start caring about politics? Why?

Once we begin to think about politics and all that comes with it, it is much more important than we often realize, regardless of our age.

How would you define politics?

Politics addresses questions such as: How do we create a more just society? How do we deal with differences? How can we work together for the common good? We all need to think about these questions because they relate to the greater call to love our neighbors.

How does politics relate to loving our neighbors?

We can love our neighbor by how we think and speak about politics. We must consider how our political thoughts and opinions affect others. The Bible teaches us to, "count others more significant" than ourselves (Phil 2:3). That includes our political thoughts. In speaking about politics, we need to be thoughtful with our words. The world is just not very good at talking about politics. If we're not careful, the bad example we see can easily become the bad example we imitate.

TWO EXTREMES TO AVOID IN ORDER TO THINK BIBLICALLY ABOUT POLITICS.

1. **Turning politics into an idol.** Our ultimate hope must be in the Lord. Politics cannot fix the deepest problem with our society—the human heart.

2. **Withdrawing from political engagement.** Why is this problematic? For one, withdrawing from politics is surrendering our call to be salt and light to the world (Matt. 5:13-16). One aspect of being salt and light is caring for those around us. Withdrawing from politics may also mean withdrawing from those who need our help the most.

FOUR KEY BIBLICAL COMMITMENTS THAT SHOULD SHAPE CHRISTIAN POLITICAL THINKING.

1. **To see the stranger as my neighbor.** Jesus told the story of the good Samaritan to indicate that we have a duty to treat our neighbors lovingly (Luke 10:29-37).

2. **To strive for the protection of every human life, regardless of race, sex, or age.**

3. **To care for the poor and marginalized.**

4. **To seek justice for all people.** Scripture calls both individuals and the state to act justly (Mic. 6:8; Ps. 72).

FOUR KEYS TO THINKING BIBLICALLY ABOUT POLITICS.

1. **Realize that every news source has a bias.**

2. **Recognize that the modern practice of politics is driven by fear and emotion.**

3. **Study all sides of an issue.**

4. **Above all, make sure you are motivated by love (1 Cor. 13:1-3).**

Day 4:
DRUGS AND ALCOHOL

"If God made everything, then why is it wrong to smoke marijuana?"

How would you answer this question?

When I was in high school, the most common answer from adults was that smoking was wrong because it was illegal. Now marijuana is legal in many states, but does that make it okay? Aren't there bigger problems for people to worry about than students smoking weed to feel good? What's the big deal?

These are great questions that we need to think about. Yet, let's consider a deeper question:

Why do you think people are so powerfully drawn to drugs, including marijuana?

Let me suggest that, at its heart, the issue is relational brokenness.

Do you agree with this? Why or why not?

Many young people turn to drugs hoping to find momentary relief from the painful reality of their daily lives. Yet I have also seen many young lives ruined, or permanently scarred, by drugs. Drugs cannot, and will not, fill the deepest desires of your heart. Only relationships with God and other people can truly offer your life meaning.

WHAT ARE SOME IMPORTANT BIBLICAL FACTORS TO CONSIDER WHEN THINKING ABOUT DRUGS AND ALCOHOL?

1. **Our bodies are a gift from God and they must be treasured as such.**

2. **Our bodies are holy for God.** For us to misuse our bodies is to bring harm to something that is not our own. Drinking, smoking, and taking drugs are wrong because they can so easily damage something that is God's property, His handiwork (see Eph. 2:10, NIV).

3. **Our minds are to love God.** Part of the greatest commandment (Mark 12:30) is to love God with our minds. Anything that pollutes our minds, such as pornography or drugs, prevents us from being able to love God in the way we are designed to.

4. **We are to be dependent on God.** So often people turn to drugs and alcohol as a way to cope with the realities of their world. This can cause an unhealthy dependency. We must depend on God and not other substances to navigate life. (**Note**: God gives us parents, friends, pastors, counselors, and legal drugs and medicine to help us in life. This is not meant to imply that we should only depend on God and not use the healthy resources He has provided us.)

How can you stand strong in avoiding drugs and alcohol? List your own ways and then consider the ways we've listed for you.

- **Choose friends wisely.** Avoid people who will encourage you to get drunk, smoke carelessly, or take drugs.

- **Avoid potentially compromising situations.** As a high school student, I promised my parents I wouldn't drink. I also would not allow a student into my car who had taken a sip of alcohol. Let me encourage you to make a similar pledge.

- **If you are taking drugs, get help from someone rather than escape your problems.** You can find freedom from this addiction. God loves you. And there are people in your life who will help. Start by sharing with a trusted adult.

Session 6

How to Love
Your Neighbor

WATCH

Use the fill-in-the-blanks and note-taking space as you watch the Session 6 teaching video together as a group.

Sean's response to the atheists: "I don't want to build _____, I want to build _____."

In our conversations with Christians and non-Christians, we need to _____

_____ _____ _____.

> **Read Matthew 22:37 (NIV).**

"Jesus replied: "'Love the Lord your God with all your heart and with all your soul and with all your mind.' "

Four steps to think biblically about everything:

Step 1: What do you _____? (Prov. 18:13)

It's more important to _____ than to _____ _____.

Step 2: _____ do you believe it? (Prov. 20:5)

Step 3: What do we have _____ _____? (Prov. 24:3)

Step 4: Where do we _____ and _____?

Final challenge:

Stand firm on _____.

Teaching videos are available at lifeway.com/thinkbiblically

GROUP DISCUSSION

Have you ever had a conversation about one of the issues we've covered in this study go badly? If so, would you mind sharing it with the group?

What do you wish you could have said or done differently?

If you reflect for a moment, I bet you all can think of a painful conversation that did not go as you intended. To be honest, I can think of a lot (and many were my fault)!

When conversations go poorly, there can be a temptation to avoid them in the future. After all, who wants to get into an argument? Aren't we told to avoid discussing politics and religion? We have considered some deeply controversial issues in this study. Given the sensitive nature of issues such as race, gender, and gun control, is it really worth entering into conversations with people about them, especially if you might get labeled a "bigot" or "intolerant"?

What do you think? Why do we enter conversations we know might end badly or with us being labeled something we're not?

Here's my answer: We must be willing to have these difficult conversations with Christians and non-Christians alike. Being disengaged is not an option for followers of Jesus. We must be willing to speak truth uncompromisingly and do so with kindness. This study has given you examples of Christians who live and speak biblical truth and who are motivated by love and compassion. That's what we need today more than ever! Will that be you?

As we approach the end of this study, how confident do you feel in engaging in difficult conversations?

You might recall the example I shared in session one, "How Do I Love My Neighbor?" about my "atheist encounter," where I role-play an atheist to Christian audiences. Sadly, there are often some critical and harsh responses aimed at my atheist character.

Think back to that lesson. Why were these Christians so harsh and critical even though they knew that the "atheist encounter" was just a role-play situation?

One reason for this is because many Christians have not thought about what and why they believe what they believe. Many lack depth in their convictions so when I challenge them, they get defensive. One goal of this study is to give you the confidence to have conversations with people who see the world differently. If you have stayed with me this far then you have enough knowledge to engage in meaningful conversations. Don't get overconfident, because there is much more to learn, but don't underestimate yourself either.

Which topics do you feel most confident in discussing with others?

Which topics do you feel inspired to learn about more?

A second reason some Christians get defensive at my atheist role play is because they don't have a loving heart toward others. They are more interested in sounding smart, or proving a point, than truly loving other people. I hope that is not you. Above all, Scripture calls us to love God and love other people. That's why we're here!

> **Read 1 Corinthians 13:1-3 (NIV).**

If I speak in the tongues of men or of angels, but do not have love, I am only a resounding gong or a clanging cymbal. If I have the gift of prophecy and can fathom all mysteries and all knowledge, and if I have a faith that can move mountains, but do not have love, I am nothing. If I give all I possess to the poor and give over my body to hardship that I may boast, but do not have love, I gain nothing.

It's impressive to speak in tongues and prophesy. But what does Paul say is most important?

Does it do any good to win an argument if you did not treat the person with love? No! Paul said if you have prophetic powers, or faith that moves mountains, but don't have love, then you are nothing. If you give away all you have, including your own life, but aren't motivated by love, then you gain nothing.

Remember, the goal of a conversation is not to sound smart. It's not to be right. The point is to learn something and love someone. Love certainly requires speaking the truth, in the right time and right manner, but our greatest goal in engaging others must always be to love them, period. It's ultimately about them learning and hearing the truth from God, not us.

Think about someone in your life who holds a different viewpoint than you or is living a lifestyle you don't agree with. How can you better love that person?

It's also important to have realistic expectations. Even if you can muster the courage to have a difficult conversation with someone, don't expect them to change their mind immediately! Some topics such as the LGBTQ conversation are matters of behavior, the nature of relationships, and personal identity. While the following passage is specifically about salvation and spiritual growth, I think the main principle it discusses can apply to discussing controversial cultural issues as well:

> **Read 1 Corinthians 3:6-8 (NIV).**

I planted the seed, Apollos watered it, but God has been making it grow. So neither the one who plants nor the one who waters is anything, but only God, who makes things grow. The one who plants and the one who waters have one purpose, and they will each be rewarded according to their own labor.

What does it mean for Paul to "plant" and Apollos to "water"?

Who is ultimately responsible for causing the seed to grow?

How does this apply to having important conversations with others?

We all have a different role to play in sharing the gospel. Some do the initial planting in others' lives while some do the watering. But ultimately God causes the seed of the gospel to grow in someone's heart.

How does this take the pressure off you when sharing the gospel or having difficult conversations?

We shouldn't expect people to immediately accept the gospel or to automatically change their minds on issues that deeply matter to them. We simply need to be faithful in doing our part. Maybe we plant a seed, causing someone to rethink their position on a topic for the first time. Maybe we continue watering the seed someone else has planted. Changing a person's mind or heart is a process, one that may require a lot of time, prayer, and love.

Do you have any final thoughts or comments as we close our study?

I am honored you have stayed with me to the end of the study. Kudos for caring about having a deep faith and about learning how to engage those around you in thoughtful conversations on challenging topics.

Here is my final challenge: Speak the truth in love. Don't buy the lie that love involves softening truth. Or the other lie that callously and thoughtlessly sharing the truth is always loving. Jesus said it is truth that sets us free. And yet, we must not speak truth without genuine concern for and understanding of others. It's not truth or love— it's truth and love. Sharing the truth so that it will be heard and received requires deep thoughtfulness and discernment.

If you follow this example of Jesus, I am confident God can use you to make a genuine difference in the lives of other people. Go for it!

Day 1:
KNOWING GOD'S WILL

One of the most common questions I receive from young Christians is, "How can I know the will of God for my life?" To be honest, this question deeply troubled me for many years. What does God want from me? What if I miss God's will? For several difficult years I viewed God's will as being hidden—like an encoded message on a treasure map. While other people seemed to have a confidence about knowing God's will, I felt no such assurance.

> **What element of discovering God's will for your life have you found to be the most challenging?**

Knowing God's will is no longer a problem for me and it should not be for you either. There are a few biblical principles I have learned about the will of God that have transformed how I make decisions.

> **What is your normal process for making a decision?**

If you read all the passages in the Bible that mention "the will of God" or "God's will," you will discover that they fall into two broad categories.

- **First, God has a moral will for us, which involves us living the way He has designed us to live.**

- **Second, God has a sovereign will, which stems from His total control of the universe. God is sovereignly moving everything toward His desired ends.**

Unless God reveals it to us, we don't know God's sovereign will, but God has revealed His moral will.

Let's consider five truths about God's moral will for your life. God's will is that you:

1. **Be saved (1 Tim. 2:4).**

2. **Be filled with the Holy Spirit (Gal. 5:16-24).**

3. **Be pure (1 Thess. 4:3).**

4. **Submit to proper authorities (1 Pet. 2:18).**

5. **Trust Him when you suffer (1 Pet. 3:17).**

   Has your idea of the will of God changed? If so, how?

What about His individual will for your life? Here's the surprising truth: The Bible does not teach that God has a hidden will for your life that you need to uncover before making decisions.

Then how do you choose a college, career, or spouse? The answer is found in seeking wisdom.

Proverbs 16:16 says, "How much better to get wisdom than gold! To get understanding is to be chosen rather than silver."

God does not make choices for us. He has given us the freedom to decide, which means we get to live with the consequences.

God cares most about who we are. If we focus on being the person God wants us to be, making the big decisions of life will become clearer and easier because God has instilled His character in our lives, which will then guide our decision-making process.

Remember, if you are believer in Jesus, God is with you no matter what decisions you make. And He is sovereignly working all things together for good of those who love Him and are called according to His purpose (Rom. 8:28).

Day 2:
DISCERNMENT

In 1 Kings 3, we see how God appeared to King Solomon in a dream and offered to give Solomon anything he wanted.

> **Take a moment and read 1 Kings 3.**

What would you ask for?

Solomon didn't ask for fame, fortune, beauty, or strength. He asked for wisdom. God granted Solomon's request, making him the wisest man who ever lived.

At the end of our last study, we looked at Proverbs 16:16: "How much better to get wisdom than gold! To get understanding is to be chosen rather than silver."

Why do you think gaining wisdom is so important?

There are countless examples of CEOs, politicians, celebrities, and even pastors who have made foolish decisions and ruined their lives. They had wealth, power, and fame and squandered it. This just shows how fleeting these things are. Nothing is more important than gaining wisdom.

Write down the name of the wisest person in your life.

How do you think he or she became so wise?

How do you think we get wisdom?

THREE WAYS TO GAIN WISDOM:

1. **Pray.** We should turn to God and His Word for wisdom. God promises that He will supply wisdom generously to anyone who lacks it (Jas. 1:5).

2. **Seek counsel from others.** Proverbs 15:22 says, "Without counsel plans fail, but with many advisers they succeed."

   What is a life lesson you learned the hard way?

   How could the situation have turned out differently had you sought or listened to someone's advice?

3. **Research.** As we've mentioned throughout this study, it's critical that we research all sides of an issue before reaching a conclusion. There can be something we've overlooked, and it's possible that our initial position was wrong. Don't make an important decision before doing your research.

In the sessions discussing important cultural topics, we saw that the Bible doesn't always give clear-cut answers to every issue. Likewise, when facing difficult decisions, God does not always tell us what to do a booming voice.

Why doesn't God tell us how to make every choice?

Remember what we learned last session: God does not have a hidden will for you to seek in making every life decision. God is more concerned with the type of person you are becoming and how that shapes the way you love Him and others. God's will is that you are conformed to the image of His Son.

Day 3:
WHAT DOES IT MEAN TO BE A GOOD LISTENER?

Have you ever felt like someone wants to tell you what he or she believes, but is not interested in hearing what you believe? Doesn't feel good, does it?

Read Proverbs 18:13.

If one gives an answer before he hears, it is his folly and shame.

Why is it foolish to respond to someone before listening?

Good listening is a way of loving people. Poor listening is a way of dismissing them. It is also a surefire way to jump to conclusions and misrepresent someone else's view. You may end up arguing against something they don't actually believe! So, before you respond to someone, make sure you listen carefully to what they say, do your best to understand it, and only then respond with grace and love.

Read Proverbs 20:5.

The purpose in a man's heart is like deep water, but a man of understanding will draw it out.

What do you think this verse means?

What are ways we can "draw out" the purpose in people's hearts?

People have deep reasons for their beliefs. Some are intellectual, but many are emotional or relational. Many people form opinions or adopt beliefs based on painful experience. For example, a teen immigrant recently shared her views on immigration with me and how they were deeply shaped by her life experience. Can you see how her experience deeply impacted her views on immigration? The same can be true with someone's views on race, gun control, and any other issue. If we respond before we understand why a person holds certain views, we may inflict more pain. But we can be part of the healing when we listen and care first.

What is an opinion you hold based on your life experience?

Is your view biblically thought out? Explain.

There's also a practical benefit to listening before responding: it's easier to listen than to respond! Listening requires little effort while responding properly requires careful thought. There's a relational benefit to listening, in that it shows the other person you care. As we've learned throughout this study, it's so important to form healthy relationships with others. There's no better way to form a relationship than by simply listening to someone.

Bottom line: Listen well, and don't respond before you understand. Now, understanding someone's position well may require asking thoughtful questions. That will be the topic of our final day.

Day 4:
A PRACTICAL GUIDE TO CONVERSATIONS

As we conclude this study, I hope you're thinking, "Okay, I want to have conversations with people about issues that matter. But where do I start?" In my experience, I have found that most people are willing to have civil conversations with others if we ask good questions and treat them respectfully.

> **What are some good "ice breaker" questions to help begin thoughtful conversations in a non-confrontational way? List a few in the space provided below.**

Here are four practical questions I regularly use in my conversations with others.[1] You can apply this approach to all the issues in this book, and more. I often use this approach in spiritual conversations with skeptics as well.

1. **What does the person believe?** A great place to start a conversation is by finding out what the other person actually believes. How is this done? Simple: listen and ask questions.

2. **Why does the person believe it?** Once we understand what the person believes, the next step is to find out why they believe it. The best way to find out is to simply ask! Since assumptions and guesses are often wrong, why not simply say, "Thanks for sharing your views on [immigration, race, gender, etc.]. Can you share with me why you hold that view?" Then listen and try to understand. Listening and trying to understand doesn't mean you agree, it just shows you love and care for the person sharing.

3. **Where do we agree?** One of the best ways to have a meaningful conversation with someone is to find areas of agreement. Proverbs 24:3 says, "By wisdom a house is built, and by understanding it is established." Common ground helps break down walls between people and fosters understanding.

4. **Where do we disagree and why?** After I understand what someone believes, why they believe it, and have found common ground, I often shift the conversation to focus on where we disagree and why. I have found it helpful to get to the heart of an issue and clarify the reason for our disagreement.

Remember, we aren't just out to win arguments, but to love and to understand people. Once we have established a relationship with a person, then he or she will be more inclined to hear what we have to say, even about the most controversial of issues.

As you close this study, take a few minutes and pray, asking God to help you engage in conversations that matter. Pray for wisdom and discernment. Pray that through showing His love to others, you can impact others for His kingdom. Write your prayer below.

Tips for Leading a Group

Thank you for your commitment to students, to loving them well and leading them into deeper relationship with God and others. The topics we cover in this study aren't easy, and we want you to know you're not alone in this. We pray for you as a leader, that you will courageously teach the truth no matter what students think. And we pray that students will grow in their understanding of God's love for them and how to think biblically through these complex issues.

PRAY

Before you meet with your group, pray. Ask God to prepare you to lead this study, and spend time praying specifically for the students in your group before every session. Ask God to prepare students to approach each session's topic with maturity and grace.

PREPARE

Don't wing the group sessions; come to group time prepared. Students will likely have questions, and these are difficult topics. Complete the study and watch the videos yourself before presenting the material to students. Dig in as you preview each session, making notes and marking specific areas of focus for your group. Consider the age, maturity level, and needs of your group before diving into specific topics. Consult with church leadership and parents about any controversial questions that may be covered during group time.

REACH OUT

Encourage the students in your group to complete each day of personal study following the group sessions. Throughout the week, follow up with group members. Consider reaching out about a specific prayer request or diving further into a question a student may have been afraid to ask in front of the whole group.

EVALUATE AND CHANGE

After each session, think about what went well and what might need to change for you to effectively lead the study. If students seem hesitant to open up, consider placing them into smaller groups as they discuss the video and content together.

SESSION 1: HOW TO TAKE A STAND

ICEBREAKER

This study requires openness and honesty, so take a few minutes to get to know the students and help them get to know one another. Laughter is often a good way to help students relax. Before your group meeting, get five envelopes and place in each of them a "Which Would You Rather?" question. Pick funny questions like, "Would you rather only listen to the same ten songs or watch the same five movies for the rest of your life?" or "Would you rather go without shampoo or toothpaste for the rest of your life?" Pick five students to open the envelopes and answer the questions.

Debrief: Thankfully we don't have to make choices like these questions asked today, but that doesn't mean we aren't faced with difficult choices. In this session, we will talk about how we are faced with challenging moral choices and how we can take a stand for what is right.

WATCH

Encourage students to follow along with the Session 1 video teaching by turning to page 9 and filling in the blanks and taking notes as Sean teaches.

DISCUSS

Use the Group Discussion section on page 10 to guide conversation with your group, digging deeper into answering the question "How can I take a stand?" Don't feel obligated to ask all the questions; use what works best for your group and let the discussion go where it needs to go. Here are the key takeaways:

- **Every day you face moral choices. How you respond to them reflects who you are right now and shapes who you will become.**

- **Even though you are a young Christian, God can use you to make a difference.**

- **God not only expects you to stand up for what is right, He will empower you with the strength to do so.**

- Even before Daniel knew the outcome, he determined he was going to honor God, and not eat the king's food. Determining that you want to honor the Lord before moral challenges come is important for standing strong today.

- You have to choose to make a stand, no one can choose for you. If you do, there is no promise that your life will be easier.

Talking Tip: Standing for what is right might cost us personally, like it did in the case of Jaelene, but we never walk alone. The Lord is with us in the high and the low moments.

TOUGH QUESTIONS

This session explored two real-world examples of facing difficult choices. In one scenario, the end result was positive. In the other, the end result was difficult for the believer who made the right choice. In this section we are trying anticipate what thoughts and questions students might have during this session. Take some time to think through these and ponder how you would answer these questions.

- Wouldn't it be better for Jaelene to wear the jersey and stay on the team so that she would have a bigger platform for the gospel?

- I can't relate to the story about Daniel. How does this connect to my life?

- I'm the only Christian in my family/friend group. If I choose to follow God, does that mean I have to turn against my family/friends?

Talking Tip: Students can ask some difficult questions. Don't feel like you have to know it all. However, your answers should always be delivered in love and kindness and with thought and care. We never know what is going on in a student's home and life that they are not telling anyone else. Being a Christian today is hard (I don't have to tell you that!), but God is with us. We cannot know how every situation will play out; the best we can do is try to honor God in every circumstance and let Him determine the outcomes. Daniel lived in a very different day and age, but his decision could have easily been seen as defiance and could have cost him his life. Chances are our lives won't be at stake, but we can lose other things that are costly (just ask Jaelene). When we give our lives to Jesus, we follow Him over everyone—including family and friends. We still must honor our parents and be kind to others, but our ultimate allegiance lies with God. That means there may be times He calls us to take a stand that makes us unpopular, costs us a position, or even brings about pain in our lives. That doesn't mean He's not with us; it just means we have to lean more closely into Him. He never betrays our trust and He never abandons us.

PRAY

- **Wrap up by praying for your group. Pray specifically that they would trust God and humbly take a stand for what is right when they are faced with tough choices.**

- **Remind students to complete the four days of personal study for Session 1 before the next group session.**

- **Encourage students to take their time with the questions, even if they don't feel like they have all the right answers.**

- **Make sure to connect with any students who may have further questions.**

SESSION 2: RELATIONSHIPS

ICEBREAKER

This session is about relationships. Bring a deck of cards to your group meeting and as students enter, let them draw a card from the deck. Start off by having students group up by color (red, black). Then have them perform an easy task like standing in order from shortest to tallest. Then have them break down into smaller groups based on suit (hearts, spades, clubs, diamonds). Give them another task, such as to get in line in order of birthday in 30 seconds. Finally, have them get together only with people who have the same number or type of card. Most students will be alone at this point. Now see which student or group can hold the longest sustained musical note (it doesn't have to be pretty). If a group has more than one person in it, when one person finishes, the next can begin.

Debrief: Some of these activities were easier with bigger groups and some were more challenging. People make life easier and more difficult, but relationships are of vital importance. That is what we are going to talk about today: how to think biblically about relationships and how they impact our lives.

WATCH

Encourage students to follow along with the Session 2 video teaching by turning to page 23 and filling in the blanks and taking notes as Sean teaches.

DISCUSS

Use the Group Discussion section on page 24 to guide conversation with your group, digging deeper into relationships. Here are the key takeaways:

- **The Bible teaches that humans have immense value because we were created in the image of God. Even when we were still sinners, God sent Jesus to die for us.**

- **Trying to fill our hearts with anything other than our relationship with God and healthy relationships with others will only leave us broken and hurting in the end.**

- **There are many relational counterfeits that vie for our hearts: consumerism, busyness, pornography, social media, video games, etc.**

- **We develop healthy relationships by finding common ground and becoming a good listener.**

- **We see the effects in our society when people do not love and are not loved by others.**

Talking Tip: No matter how students feel about themselves, it is important to always remind them that God loves them so much that He sent His only Son for them (John 3:16). Having healthy relationships with others begins by having a healthy relationship with God.

TOUGH QUESTIONS

Jonathan modeled real friendship toward David in that he was selfless and self-sacrificing. Ultimately, God reveals the greatest example of love through Jesus. Still, students might have some challenging thoughts or questions about the content in today's study, such as:

- **Why are you always railing against stuff we love, like social media and video games?**

- **Are all people made in God's image? What about terrible people like Hitler and Osama bin Laden? Surely it's okay to hate them, right?**

- **How can someone be my neighbor when we have absolutely nothing in common and don't agree on anything? How am I supposed to love that person?**

Talking Tip: This session explored the importance of relationships and what happens when people do not love or are not loved. Sadly, there might be students in your group who do not feel loved—not at home, school, or maybe even at church. There may even be relational stress in your group that makes this discussion uncomfortable. Let me challenge you to do the hard work. Talk about it, but do so in love and kindness. If things get out of hand, deescalate the situation, but don't ignore what's happening. The point of this session is to make it evident that we need healthy relationships with each other and with God. That begins by grasping our standing before God. When we see ourselves in the right light before Him as sinners saved by grace, turned into saints who sin from time to time, we can then more rightly relate to each other. Genuine, authentic relationships are built through hard work, understanding, grace, and forgiveness. We are called to love all people as Jesus first loved us. That doesn't mean we agree with everyone, just that we treat everyone with dignity, kindness, and respect, just like we would want to be treated.

PRAY

- **Wrap up by praying for your group. Pray specifically that they would pursue healthy relationships with others and look for places where broken relationships can be healed by the love of Jesus.**

- **Remind students to complete the four days of personal study for Session 2 before the next group session.**

- **Make sure to connect with any students who may have further questions.**

SESSION 3: SEX

ICEBREAKER

This session is about sex. Sometimes it's hard to talk about sex because it's awkward or embarrassing. Find the board game "Catch Phrase" where a person tries to get the other people on his or her team to guess a word without saying a few important words. If you cannot find the game, recreate the game yourself. For example, if a person were trying to get someone to say "Bird" they might not be allowed to say, wings, eggs, nest, beak, or fly. Divide your group into smaller groups, depending on size, and allow each team to try and guess the word twice. Give each team 30 seconds to guess the word.

Debrief: It's hard to talk about something when we can't use certain words. Today, we are going to talk about sex. It can be embarrassing and awkward but it is such an important topic because the world sees sex so much differently than what the Bible teaches. If we are going to think biblically about sex, we're going to have to cut through the awkwardness and embarrassment and talk about it plainly and openly, not mincing words. Let's pledge to each other today that we'll be mature about this and leave the snickering and jokes behind.

WATCH

Encourage students to follow along with the Session 3 video teaching by turning to page 37 and filling in the blanks and taking notes as Sean teaches.

DISCUSS

Use the Group Discussion section on page 38 to guide conversation with your group, digging deeper into the Bible's teaching on sex. Here are the key takeaways:

- **Even in such a sex-saturated world, God desires for you to follow His plan for sex, gender, and marriage. His standards haven't changed, even if the world's have.**

- **Since God is our Creator, we are going to have to trust His instructions on sex, gender, and marriage, even if His instructions don't make sense to us or the outside world.**

- Not only is God good, but His commands are for our good. We may not understand all of God's instructions about sex, but He has proven Himself trustworthy—most clearly through the gift of Jesus.

- God's plans for sex, gender, and marriage are not meant to steal our fun, but to help us flourish in our relationships with our spouse and others.

- We only experience real freedom when we follow the loving plan of our Creator who knows us best and designed us with purpose.

Talking Tip: Let's be real. Your students are probably feeling pressed on every side to conform to a worldly perspective on sex. Following a biblical worldview on sex has probably labeled them narrow-minded at best and a hateful bigot at worst among their peers. But, throwing rocks at the world never changed their hearts. We have to handle this conversation with compassion, love, grace, sympathy, and kindness.

TOUGH QUESTIONS

These questions are taken directly from the study. There are good answers to these questions in the study, particularly in exploring the sexual ethic of Jesus and how much better the world would be if everyone followed it.

- **Is sexual activity really that big a deal?**

- **Does porn really hurt anyone?**

- **As long as sex is consensual, there's nothing wrong with it, right?**

- **Why embrace a view of sex, love, and gender that seems closed-minded?**

- **Isn't the Christian sexual ethic unrealistic today anyway?**

Talking Tip: This topic is sensitive so it's a good idea to make sure parents know that these topics will be covered and discussed. It's also important that if a student confides in you or the group that they have feelings or experiences contrary to God's design that you take further steps. As already stated, sensitivity, kindness, grace, and love must be expressed at all times, but it is important to walk with students and their parents or guardians and refer them to experienced biblical counselors or those more qualified to provide the help necessary.

PRAY

- Wrap up by praying for your group. Pray specifically that they would know in their hearts the goodness of God and trust His instructions are for their good—especially when it comes to sex, love, gender, and marriage.

- Remind students to complete the four days of personal study for Session 3 before the next group session. This week explores more aspects of God's design for sex and love.

- Make sure to connect with any students who may have further questions.

SESSION 4: CARE

ICEBREAKER

Search YouTube or the internet for a video titled "Moonwalking Bear Awareness Test" and show it to your students (try to make sure they don't see the title of the video so the punchline isn't ruined). In this video a team of basketball players pass a ball to each other as another team passes as well, weaving in and out and among each other. After a few seconds the video will ask "how many times did the team in white pass the basketball?" Pause at that point and let students answer. After they respond, show them the rest of the video. As the players are moving around the screen passing the ball, a person dressed in a bear costume moonwalks right through the middle of the screen and no one will even notice.

Debrief: How did this happen? How did this bear moonwalk right through the middle of the screen and we didn't even notice? Because we were focused on something else. Today we are going to talk about care, how we care for others in spite of our differences. I think we'll find if we only focus on ourselves and our own opinions, we might miss the bigger picture, like a bear moonwalking right through the middle of the screen.

WATCH

Encourage students to follow along with the Session 4 video teaching by turning to page 51 and filling in the blanks and taking notes as Sean teaches.

DISCUSS

Use the Group Discussion section on page 52 to guide conversation with your group, digging deeper into the Bible's teaching on care. Here are the key takeaways:

- **James 1:19 says to be quick to hear and slow to speak. We should focus on asking more questions, and aiming to understand, rather than feeling the need to have an opinion on every issue.**

- **Just because you are young, does not mean you can't influence your family and friends. It may not even be due to your vast knowledge, but simply because you are loving and respectful.**

- **Showing thought and care in your words will make it more likely for others to consider your opinions on an issue.**

- **The Bible does not specifically address many pressing issues in our world today, but there are principles we can apply to help guide our thoughts and hearts on important matters.**

Talking Tip: It is very possible there are a variety of opinions on some of the topics that are covered in this chapter. Some students may feel very strongly one way or the other about gun control. The point is not to definitively say, "This is what the Bible says about gun control" but to help students filter their opinions about gun control (and other hot button issues) through the Bible rather than vice versa.

TOUGH QUESTIONS

Like many issues, students opinions are probably shaped by their personal experiences, parents, and friends. If a student has parents who were immigrants, chances are they will feel much differently about immigration than a student whose family has lived in this country for generations. Take some time and think about these questions students might ask in regard to this session:

- **What do I do if I have an opinion on a topic that is different from my parents?**

- **Is there only one way to see an issue like climate change?**

- The Bible has nothing to say about so many of these issues because they didn't exist then. How can it help me understand or know how to feel and think about these important subjects?

Talking Tip: For many topics, believe it or not, there is not only one way to see it. There can be many different points of view. The important point is that we filter our views and opinions through Scripture, not the other way around. People may see these topics differently, but how we treat one another in discussing them is of far more value. The point is, life is sacred and we are all created in the image of God, so even if someone disagrees on how to view something, we treat each other with care and we love like Jesus loves us.

PRAY

- Wrap up by praying for your group. Pray specifically that they would learn to listen first and speak second. Pray that students would learn to express their opinions with love and care.

- Remind students to complete the four days of personal study for Session 4 before the next group session. This week explores some topics many have different opinions on. These days will help students to process them from a biblical point of view.

- Make sure to connect with any students who may have further questions.

SESSION 5: CULTURE

ICEBREAKER

Start your session with a game of "This One or That One." For this game, come up with two different items that are in the same category and instruct the students in your group to choose which one they prefer by going to one side of the room or the other. For example, for the category of social media, ask them to choose between TikTok and Instagram. For the category of energy drinks, ask them to choose between Monster or Red Bull. Come up with two options for several more categories, such as comic book movie franchise (Marvel or DC), smartphone brand (iPhone or Samsung), music style (hip-hop or country).

Debrief: Many of the things you just chose are fun entertainment like music and movies. Others can be useful things, like cell phones and social media. In this session we are going to explore things in our culture that have an impact on our lives, like entertainment, politics, and social media. Some of these things are morally neutral and some are not, but how we use all of them and the place we allow them to have in our lives matters a great deal.

WATCH

Encourage students to follow along with the Session 5 video teaching by turning to page 65 and filling in the blanks and taking notes as Sean teaches.

DISCUSS

Use the Group Discussion section on page 66 to guide conversation with your group, digging deeper into the Bible's teaching on culture. Here are the key takeaways:

- **Since we are body and soul, physical and spiritual, what we put into our bodies and what we allow into our minds both really matter, but in different ways.**

- **Social media and entertainment contain ideas that shape how we think about the world. They affect us both emotionally and intellectually. Therefore, we should "take every thought captive to obey Christ" (2 Cor. 10:5).**

- **Since politics has invaded everything in our society, we need to know how to navigate the issues wisely. We need to make sure we examine all sides of every issue, that we are pursuing truth, and not simply reinforcing what we already believe.**

- **As Christians, we must always consider what the Bible has to say on the issues, though not every issue has a clear-cut answer in Scripture. But we can always find a guiding principle if we dig deep enough.**

- **Bottom line: We must be mindful of what we allow into our bodies, and we must also consider what we allow into our minds.**

Talking Tip: It is important to have open and honest discussion on cultural matters, but the point of this session is not to devolve into a political argument. Reinforce with your group the importance of being open to listen to all sides of an argument, then let the Bible and its teachings inform how you formulate your opinion.

TOUGH QUESTIONS

For some people, there is a temptation to think that a Christian can only vote one way and for one party, but that is just not true. Many devoted followers of Jesus vote in many different ways in every election. You might find that students are more open minded in some areas, but more closed minded in others. Take some time and think about these questions that students might ask in regard to this session:

- **How long is too long to spend on social media?**

- **Should I watch an R-rated movie?**

- **It seems like all politicians are out just for themselves. Why should I care about politics?**

- **We can agree that drinking to the point of intoxication and abusing drugs is bad and wrong. The Bible is clear on that, but what about vaping or tobacco products?**

Talking Tip: The key to all these questions is Matthew 6:33a: "Seek first the kingdom of God." This doesn't mean that everything we do or watch has to be blatantly Christian, but we should be careful with what we consume. We must use discernment and examine with honesty if what we are watching and doing is healthy for our minds and bodies. If doing something reveals itself to ultimately be unhealthy, we should not do it or approach it with caution and use it in moderation.

PRAY

- **Wrap up by praying for your group to let the Spirit inform their hearts on these matters.**

- **Remind students to complete the four days of personal study for Session 5 before the next group session. A couple of these days might step on their toes a bit, but encourage them to reflect honestly on these matters.**

- **Make sure to connect with any students who may have further questions.**

SESSION 6: HOW TO LOVE YOUR NEIGHBOR

ICEBREAKER

This is your final session together. Make sure to let the students in your group know how much you've enjoyed working through this study with them. There is a strong icebreaker question on page 80 of the Group Discussion guide. Be sure and think of an example when you've not handled a conversation about a tricky issue well and be ready to share it if students are slow to respond. Be sure and give them time to think, though. It can take a moment to come up with a response or for them to work up the courage to share their example.

Debrief: It's not easy having conversations about some of these topics. Today we are going to discuss how we can have conversations about these difficult topics well and how we can do it in a way that honors God and potentially helps others come to a biblical perspective as well.

WATCH

Encourage students to follow along with the Session 6 video teaching by turning to page 79 and filling in the blanks and taking notes as Sean teaches.

DISCUSS

Use the Group Discussion section on page 80 to guide conversation with your group, digging deeper into how we can love our neighbor best. Here are the key takeaways:

- **Being disengaged is not an option for followers of Jesus. We must be willing to speak truth uncompromisingly and do so with kindness.**

- **Many Christians have not thought about what and why they believe what they believe. Many lack depth in their convictions. Sadly, many don't have a loving attitude in their heart toward others.**

- **Love certainly requires speaking the truth, in the right time and right manner, but our greatest goal in engaging others must always be to love them, period.**

- We shouldn't expect people to immediately accept the gospel or to automatically change their minds on issues that deeply matter to them. But, we need to be faithful in doing our part.

- Speak the truth in love. Don't buy the lie that love involves softening truth. Or the other lie that callously and thoughtlessly sharing the truth is always loving.

Talking Tip: The key point students need to grasp from this session is the truth of 1 Corinthians 13:1-3. Love has to motivate our words and actions. If we do not have love, we do not have anything.

TOUGH QUESTIONS

Take some time and think about these questions that students might ask:

- **How can I love someone and still say hard things to them?**

- **How can I love someone and respond without sounding harsh or hateful?**

- **Why does it seem like the world is moving away from God so much?**

Talking Tip: For many Christians, we have lost the right to be heard by others today because our responses have not been filled with love. For most people, relationships go a long way. If we have a relationship with someone built on love, even if we disagree on important issues, they will be more willing to listen and consider a biblical point of view. When life gets hard for people who don't know Jesus, they might come to you for help if they have seen the difference Jesus has made in your life. If students can live that way and be honest about their faith in Jesus and faithful to walk with Him, they can make an impact on people who are far from God.

PRAY

- **Wrap up by praying for your group to let love season all of their conversations on the challenging topics this study has covered.**

- **Remind students that even though the Group Discussion sessions are over, they're still to complete the four days of personal study for Session 6. You might even want to go over the topics that will be covered in the study days to help encourage them to follow through.**

NOTES

NOTES

SOURCES

Session 1

1. John Stonestreet, "Breakpoint: The U.S. Women's Soccer Team and Jaelene Hinkle," June 27, 2019, https://www.breakpoint.org/breakpoint-the-u-s-womens-soccer-team-and-jaelene-hinkle/.

2. Common Sense Media, "Tweens, Teens, Tech, and Mental Health: Coming of Age In An Increasingly Digital, Uncertain, and Unequal World," July 29, 2020, https://www.commonsensemedia.org/research/tweens-teens-tech-and-mental-health, 11, 17.

3. Stopbullying.gov, "What is Bullying," U.S. Department of Health and Human Services, accessed August 25, 2020, https://www.stopbullying.gov/bullying/what-is-bullying.

4. Ibid.

Session 3

1. Ellen Dewitt, "Best-Selling Book Series of All Time," July 18, 2019, https://stacker.com/stories/3313/best-selling-book-series-all-time.

2. J.K. Rowling Writes About Her Reasons for Speaking Out on Sex and Gender Issues," June 10, 2020, https://www.jkrowling.com/opinions/j-k-rowling-writes-about-her-reasons-for-speaking-out-on-sex-and-gender-issues.

3. Abigail Shrier, *Irreversible Damage* (Washington, DC: Regnery Publishing, 2020), 3.

4. Ibid., xxiv.

5. Eric W. Owens, Richard J. Behun, Jill C. Manning, Rory C. Reid, "The Impact of Internet Pornography on Adolescents: A Review of the Research," Sexual Addiction & Compulsivity, 19:99-122, 2012.

6. "The Porn Epidemic," Josh McDowell Ministry: josh.org/resources/apologetics/research/#pornportfolio.

7. For instance, the Colson Center has some short videos responding to claims like "Porn is Victimless" https://www.youtube.com/watch?v=oYL7vRQTSR4. Or see my 2.5-minute YouTube video, "What's Wrong with Porn?" https://www.youtube.com/watch?v=oYL7vRQTSR4.

8. Mark Sherman, *AP News*, "Supreme Court Overturns Roe v. Wade; States Can Ban Abortion," June 24, 2022, https://apnews.com/article/abortion-supreme-court-decision-854f60302f21c2c35129e58cf8d8a7b0.

9. Alan Shlemon, "The S.L.E.D. Test," *Stand to Reason*, March 13, 2014, https://www.str.org/w/the-sled-test

Session 4

1. For a good list of essential Christian doctrines, see "The 99 Essential Doctrines" by The Gospel Project, https://www.gospelproject.com/wp-content/uploads/tgp2018/2018/03/99-Essentials-Booklet.pdf.

2. Emanuela Barbiroglio, "Generation Z Fears Climate Change More Than Anything Else," Forbes, December 9, 2019, https://www.forbes.com/sites/emanuelabarbiroglio/2019/12/09/generation-z-fears-climate-change-more-than-anything-else/?sh=68ad91e7501b.

3. Rebecca M. Cunningham, Maureen A. Walton, and Patrick M. Carter, "The Major Causes of Death in Children and Adolescents in the United States," The New England Journal of Medicine, December 20, 2018, https://www.ncbi.nlm.nih.gov/pmc/articles/PMC6637963/.

Session 5

1. Hannah Schwar, "How Instagram and Facebook Are Intentionally Designed to Mimic Addictive Painkillers," August 11, 2021, https://www.businessinsider.com/facebook-has-been-deliberately-designed-to-mimic-addictive-painkillers-2018-12.

2. "Social Media Addiction," *Addiction Center*, accessed June 20, 2022, https://www.addictioncenter.com/drugs/social-media-addiction.

Session 6

1. These questions were inspired from Tim Muehlhoff, "Christians in the Argument Culture: Apologetics as Conversation," in *A New Kind of Apologist*, ed. Sean McDowell (Eugene, OR: Harvest House, 2016), 21-28.

Sharing Truth With A New Generation

SeanMcDowell.org

- 🐦 Sean_McDowell
- ♪ Sean_McDowell
- 📷 SeanMcDowell
- ▶ Dr. Sean McDowell

Podcast:
The Think Biblically Podcast

Get the most from your study.

Promotional videos and other leader materials available at lifeway.com/thinkbiblically.

Students have questions. We need to help them think biblically about them. Questions like:

- How do we think biblically about pressing issues today?
- What is real justice? How do we care about poverty and racism in a way that helps people and reveals a Christlike heart?
- How do we live out a Christian worldview on issues dividing the world more than ever, such as politics, abortion, and homosexuality?
- How do we shut out cultural noise and prayerfully ask, "How would Jesus respond?"
- How do we love God and keeping His commands?

Join Sean McDowell in this six-session study as he walks students through a Christian ethic for a new generation. Discover how to discern biblical truth, real justice, and God's love amid the noise of today's world. Learn how to listen and engage in healthy dialogue when it comes to issues like race, poverty, homosexuality, immigration, social media, and politics. Most of all, learn how to show God's love to everyone by speaking truth and pointing others to the ultimate authority, Jesus.

ADDITIONAL RESOURCES

Think Biblically Video Bundle
A 6-week study with 6 video teaching sessions from Sean McDowell available on lifeway.com/thinkbiblically or on the Lifeway On Demand app.

***Think Biblically* eBook**
An eBook format of this 6-week study for students, exploring how to think biblically about today's pressing issues.

Chasing Love
A 9-session study from Sean McDowell helping students navigate sexuality, marriage, and relationships biblically.